A MEMOIR

GRANDSON
of a
SLAVE

SAMUEL CARTER

ISBN: 978-1-7341262-6-6

Carter. Samuel
Grandson of a Slave

Editors: Amy Ashby, Anurag Andra, Holly Lopez, and Uma Hayes
Editorial Assistant: Melissa Long
Researcher: Kristina Duemmler

Warren publishing

Published by Warren Publishing
Charlotte, NC
www.warrenpublishing.net
Printed in the United States

To my last living brother, Raybon Carter.

*Your leadership and the example you set have been the
key to my survival ever since I was a young boy. Your
physical and mental fortitude protected me from the
challenges of the racist South; your work ethic helped me
to gain confidence in my own abilities; your wit and humorous
personality still give me perspective and feed my own. (As you
said during a recent conversation of ours, "When you started
that book, the Grand Canyon was a cereal bowl!")*

Your life inspires me.

✿

*To my baby sister, Margaret, who passed away
unexpectedly prior to the release of this book.*

*Margaret: Not only am I devastated by your untimely passing,
I'm also deeply saddened that you did not have an opportunity
to see this collection, this flashback of memories from growing up
in Alabama in the 1940s and '50s, before heading north in the
'60s. Your life was a true blessing, and your memory a treasure.
Life on this planet will never be the same without you.*

ACKNOWLEDGMENTS

Writing this book was like drawing water from a well without a bucket. I am thankful to my family and friends for their motivation, assistance, advice, and support. Thanks to Marissa, my youngest daughter, for jump-starting my journey as an author and assisting with finding a publishing team. I am grateful for your artistic genius and willingness to contribute these talents to the photo on my cover. Thanks to Melissa, my second daughter. You have supported me beyond measure. Without you, this book would never have come to fruition. I appreciate your encouragement and mentorship.

I also want to thank Marilyn, my oldest daughter, for helping me recall impactful stories from my life, but more importantly, I want to thank you for giving me a grandson. Many thanks to that grandson, Evan, for being my inspiration to continue this journey of life in a bold fashion. Evan, I thank God for making you the human being you are today, one who is wise beyond your years.

And of course, I want to thank Raybon, my brother, for his help in reminding me of our past and of the rich family history that is so important for this book.

Thanks go out to my publisher for her inspiration and creative way of telling my story. And most important of all, I want to thank my wife, Monica, for all her help, support, wisdom, and patience. Monica, for your understanding, companionship, and the gift of our three wonderful daughters, I will always love you.

Samuel

INTRODUCTION

As I look back over my life, I can clearly see and understand how I became the man I am today. I have had so many inexplicable and wonderful experiences in my lifetime, I cannot count them all. So often, I have found myself in situations I couldn't explain, but I've been able to navigate them with patience and time. One such situation stands out, because it taught me about the gift of love, and the self-respect and freedom that can come with it.

I remember the year—1947. I was five years old, and my brother Raybon had bought me a red tricycle. He was eleven years old and worked on a farm, plowing fields to earn money. That tricycle was my first form of personal transportation. I was so excited. It gave me pride and made me feel like I was equal to everyone else. Raybon told me in later years that he had paid five dollars for the trike. Now, at that time, five dollars was a great amount of money, especially for an eleven-year-old boy. He could have used that money for more important and useful things, such as food or clothes, but he decided to give me this gift because he thought so much of me. And what a sense of freedom it gave me. At the age of five, I was free to ride from sunup to sundown. There were restrictions, of course: I couldn't ride on the roads, and I had to let my parents or a sibling know where I was at all times, or bring them with me. Still, no one else rode that bike but me.

With this experience, I learned about independence and how it felt to be *free*. Just as importantly, it taught me generosity. It taught me how to love and be loved. And that's what life is about, isn't it?

THE SEVENTEEN OF US

I come from a large family of fifteen children, ten girls and five boys. The girls were named Jessie Bell, Catherine, Eloise, Dixie Lee, Mammie Paul, Aubrey Lee, Operee, Edna Jean, Carrie Mae, and Margaret. The boys were Eugene, AC, Raybon, Huston, and me. I felt protected being in a large family.

We had great parents. My mother was a kind, loving lady. Her name was Essie Arnill May Carter and she devoted herself to her family. She was a small lady with a big heart. She was an educator and loved to read to us and tell us how all her children would know how to read; none of her children were going to be illiterate.

There were plenty of people living in our community who did not know how to read. I remember there were times when white people would bring their mail to our house, and my mother would read it to them. My mother was kind to everyone, no matter their race or color. She told us to never look down on anyone, for we were all God's children. She was well respected by her peers and, as a young boy, I watched and learned from her as I grew. She taught us to respect everyone, and if we couldn't get along with someone, we should just "feed them out of a long-handled spoon," because you can't please everyone.

My mother could also read music. We had an organ in our home where we would all gather around her, watching in awe as she played and sang songs from the hymnal. Every member of the family could sing, but my sister Edna Jean was the most gifted. Her voice would inspire the hearts of people and bring tears to their eyes.

Growing up, my sisters were very protective of me. I think it was because I was the youngest boy at that time, and they were concerned about my safety. In the 1940s, racism was at its peak in Alabama, and danger lurked everywhere. My sisters were also great leaders who cared for our family. And although they were all so different from one another, I was impressed with the character and personality of each.

My oldest sisters, Catherine, Jessie Bell, and Dixie Lee were already grown and married by the time I was born, and they'd started their own families, so I didn't see them as much.

Jessie Bell was the first daughter, the oldest of ten girls, and she was expulsive; she tended to push everyone away. She was the oldest, and the first to leave home and get married, so I didn't know her that much.

Catherine was sickly. I remember her always being sick.

Dixie Lee was pleasant, it was a joy to be in her presence. She was also a business lady; she was a hair dresser and had her own beauty shop too.

Eloise was shy, kept to herself, and didn't talk much. She was the only one of my sisters who didn't have children, and I think her childlessness led to much of her despair later in life.

Mammie Paul was a woman of faith, she was a free giver to us, and she was kind and laughable.

Aubrey Lee, who we thought of as the family matriarch, kept house and cooked. She was strong-minded, with a great determination to do what was right. She was very religious, a Christian woman.

Although she was not the oldest, Operee was gifted with leadership and wisdom. My mother put Operee in charge of the family and instructed her to watch over us. In return, I was always very watchful over Operee.

I am blessed that two of my youngest sisters are still living today. Edna Jean always had and still has a beautiful singing voice, and she's the educator in the family with a strong desire to learn. Carrie Mae is an adventurer; she's always gone about exploring things and loves to travel and live a life of freedom.

Margaret, my baby sister, passed away unexpectedly during the writing (but prior to the release) of this book. My heart is exceedingly heavy, as she was the youngest and closest to me in age. Those who knew Margaret would agree that she was vivacious and full of life; however, her most endearing quality was selflessness with an untiring dedication to service to the family. Even as a child she was a natural caretaker, always showing concern for our family. Like Carrie Mae, she was also an adventurer. I miss her.

When my sisters grew up, they learned quickly that there was no place else to go. At that time, our father was a sharecropper. Farming was his only way to make a living, and all of us who were old enough had to work on the farm to pick cotton, pull corn, or stack peanuts. We lived off the farmland, no recreation, just the cotton, corn, and peanuts—hard work from sunup to sundown.

Looking back, I can understand why some of my sisters left home at such an early age; country life on a farm was not exciting, especially for young girls. The church was the only place to socialize, so they didn't have social lives beyond church. (And even if they had, we didn't have much by way of transportation.) As budding young women, they wanted to enjoy life, even if that meant leaving home at a tender age.

⚜

It was years later when I found out the history of my family. Being a wise woman, my mother had never talked about my parents' early relationship—or my father's previous marriage—knowing it would cause hardship within the family. My father's first wife, Harriet Grimes Carter, had died many years earlier, leaving him with five young children to raise, all girls.

It's distressing for me to reflect upon the agony, pain, and misery my father must have had to endure. His world had been so suddenly invaded with fear and vexation, helplessness and despair; terror and panic had taken hold of his home. There he was with five daughters to raise, a difficult task for any man, but especially in the 1920s, and he lacked the skills or competence to do so. Jessie Bell was nine, Catherine was seven, Eloise was six, Dixie was four, and Mammie Paul was just eleven months old when their mother passed away. It was a low point in our father's life, grieving from the loss of his wife, the mother of his children; his heart was filled with emptiness and desolation.

Shortly after, he met my mother, Essie Arnell May, a beautiful young woman of high class, both intellectually and morally. She was a lady with good character, and well respected within the community. My mother had a way of meekness about herself and cared about the well-being of others.

It was January 29, 1929, a cold day, when they got married in Pigeon Creek, a small town in Butler County near Greenville, Alabama. My mother was twenty-three years old and did not have children when she married my father. She had been single, living her life with her parents at home. To my thinking, it was a mystery how my father persuaded my mother to marry him with *five* children to take care of. I wondered if her father had told her to marry him, seeing that my father was a good, young man, also well respected in the community, and was in a desperate situation with his children. Or perhaps it was that my father, being the handsome man he was, charmed her with his good looks and comely personality.

All I know is that whatever he said or did, it worked.

There had been no wedding bells, no honeymoon, when my parents married. My mother found herself faced with a big responsibility: mother to five young girls from my father's previous wife. The girls were still so small, Mammie Paul being too young to remember anything about their biological mother. Growing up, I never heard my older sisters talk about their mother, in fact, I was eighteen years old before I learned we had different mothers. At that point, I wondered if they had ever longed to see her again. Did their hearts ache for her?

My mother became their mother by caring for them as her own. She put herself to the task of making things better and comforting them, knowing the crisis they had experienced. She was solely concerned for their needs, their problems, and her relationship with each child.

One year and six months later, my mother had her first child, Aubrey Lee, another girl. Dad was so sad and disappointed, because he'd wanted a son. He'd told my mother before they had their first child, "Essie, when we have our first child, I'm going to give him or her my name." When the baby was born, it was a girl, so my dad named her Aubrey (and added the middle name, "Lee," "because she was a girl").

It was a hard time for my mother after the birth of Aubrey Lee, as she was now burdened with two babies to care for at the same time—one of them a newborn. She had no help; the girls were too young to cook, wash clothes, or clean the house, and still needed to be cared for.

As they grew up, my oldest sisters made a decision to make better lives for themselves. My mother had fulfilled her responsibilities by raising them, and developing their characters as young women with moral qualities. At that time, the social environment of the South was in turmoil— especially for young black women. Given the stress of working in the fields with no social lives, it was a real crisis for them; as budding young women, they wanted to enjoy life.

Jessie Bell and Catherine left home at fifteen and sixteen years old, respectively, and started their families. In their minds, they were already stable and equipped to make decisions of their own and determine their futures. And

Dixie Lee, when she was just thirteen, asked our father if she could go and spend the summer with our cousin who lived in Florida. Our father let her, she left, and it was many years before she came back. She married a man named Davis, and they had a son named Felix.

Years later, when Dixie finally came back to see us, we were so excited to see her and to meet Davis and Felix. My father was extremely glad to know she was well—and alive. He'd never heard a word from her after she'd left.

We didn't know where any of my sisters went most of the time. They just went.

Those were dreadful times for my father, not knowing where his daughters were, not hearing from them for long periods of time. It scared him and saddened him that his girls had left, and at such young ages; they were too young to defend themselves and too immature to make the right choices for their own welfare.

🌿

My father's name was Aubrey Carter. He was very protective of us and cared for his family at all costs. He was brave and fearless and made sure none of us were taken advantage of, the same way his father had been. My father's father, Grandpa Nute, had been a slave. Family was sacred to him. As a slave, his life had been impermanent, and family was not a guarantee. It was not something to take for granted. When Grandpa Nute eventually started his own family, his need to protect them, to hold on to them and not let them go, drove all his other actions. That was the key lesson he passed down to my father.

What I remember most about my father are the stories he used to tell and how we would always laugh together. There aren't a lot of funny stories I remember about my father, but I do remember he was a social chameleon—he was great at adapting to different environments and talking to people from all walks of life. I like to think I learned my people skills from him. He was a charismatic man.

A fond memory I have of my father stemmed from a crazy situation that happened over sixty years ago—around about 1957. My best friend from school, Willie Stevens, brought this story up again when we spoke recently. It was late one evening, about seven o'clock. We were coming back from a little town called Greenville, about fifteen miles from where we lived in the country. Willie and I had gone with my father who had some personal business to take care of with one of his associates there.

On the way home, I drove. At just fifteen years old, I didn't have a driver's license at that time, but my father had given me permission to drive because he knew I was an excellent driver. So, all three of us were sitting in the front seat of my father's black 1950, four-door Buick. I was the driver, Willie was in the middle, and my father was at the passenger side. That was when I did something unwise. There was a car in front of us driving pretty slowly, but the road was really curvy, so I passed the car in the middle of a curve. Turns out, it was an unmarked police car. The officer turned on his flashing lights and siren. I said to myself, "Oh hell, I done a stupid thing!" I should've known better.

I held my breath, terrified. Then I slowed down, pulled to the side of the highway, and just before the car came to a complete stop, I leapt from the driver's seat into the back of the car, head first. To this day, it's a mystery to me how I did that. Meanwhile, my father climbed past Willie to get into the driver's seat and stop the car.

Well, the police saw them cross each other, but he had not seen me jump into the back. That officer thought Willie had been driving the car and pulled out his handcuffs to take Willie to jail, but my father stopped him. He said, "I was driving this car. Here is my license, this boy was not driving. I'll meet you downtown tomorrow and we'll clear up this matter."

Willie and I bit our tongues, trying not to laugh. The officer just said, "Okay," got in his car, and took off. We continued home … with my father doing the driving.

Four or five years ago, my sister Margaret ran into Willie Stevens at a class reunion in Alabama and got his phone number. It turned out he was living in Columbia, South Carolina, not too far from where I now live in Charlotte. We caught up and were so glad to speak to each other. The first thing Willie asked me on the phone was, "After all them years, there's one thing I need to know, Sam. How did you get into that back seat?" I laughed and said, "I don't know how I got in that back seat, but I knew my dad would bail us out." Reuniting with Willie has been such a joy, and we have stayed in touch with each other. We call each other weekly and talk about things from our childhood.

❧

My father was always there for us. He was a great father—and a great farmer. He was also a deacon at the church we attended and was a wonderful singer. He was a biblical scholar; he read his Bible each day, read it with great piety.

Us children were not allowed to make any noise when he was reading; we had to be quiet or go outside. Our father wanted to concentrate, so we respected his wishes. He knew a lot about scripture, sometimes even more than the preacher. People would ask him questions about the Bible, and he would always have an answer. Reading the Bible was his hobby; he would read it daily.

He taught Sunday school every second and fourth Sunday of the month. The church was seen as the heartbeat of the community, so any man who held a role in the church was therefore a pillar of that community. Everything happened at church. At that time, the church was the only institution in the black community with concern and compassion to liberate the people—socially, knowledgeably, and spiritually.

My father was proud of all his sons. He had always wanted a son so badly, but his first six children had been daughters. When Eugene, my oldest brother, was finally born, my father was especially proud of him. Not that he cared any less for the rest of us, but Eugene was his first-born son. Every father wants a son. To fathers, sons are the next great adventure. Eugene was smart, brave, and a hard worker too—always working on the farm and in the woods, sawing logs with my father. But Eugene had his weaknesses. He loved to drink whiskey and moonshine, which my father disapproved of.

The next oldest son was AC. Like Eugene, he was smart, brave, and high-tempered, but AC was also mean and only loved our mother. Raybon once told me that when AC got angry, his eyes would turn red and he'd lose control of himself. According to Raybon, one day AC was working in the woods, cutting timber with my father, Eugene, and Raybon, when Mr. Von Jones, the landowner, approached AC. Jones was a white man, six feet tall, who weighed about two hundred pounds. Out of nowhere, Mr. Jones started screaming at AC in a rude and disrespectful manner. Mr. Jones had never acted like that before; it may have been that he'd had a bad night at home with his wife, but he took it out on AC … and it almost cost Mr. Von Jones his life. AC grabbed an axe and ran at the man with the intent to kill. Fortunately, Raybon and my father were able to tackle AC to the ground. Mr. Jones just stood frozen in front of a tree. My father immediately rounded up the boys and took them home. They never worked for Mr. Jones again.

AC died at the young age of twenty-one. He had been riding one of our father's mules, and he fell off onto the pavement, which caused a terrible bruise on his left leg. The bruise later developed gangrene, and his leg had to be amputated. He died shortly after. That was one of the saddest times our family ever went through.

Raybon, the middle child of five sons, has always been gifted. He grew up tall, dark, and with a head full of hair. He's always been a ladies' man, and my father had to keep his eyes on him when we were growing up. Still, Dad always knew he could count on Raybon; he trusted him, and I do too. Ever since we were kids, Raybon has taught me everything I need to know about life. He's never been a church-goer, but he's the best Christian I know, and he has the ability to make people laugh.

Huston, the next to youngest, was a protector with great physical strength. I remember when we went swimming, we could ride on Huston's back; he was such a good swimmer.

He was more reserved, wise in his decision making but bold in action. It was Huston and Raybon who bought our first family car in 1950, when Huston was just fourteen years old.

Then there was me, the youngest of the boys. In the Bible, Jacob speaks about his sons and describes each one's character. He said, "One was weak as water," and so forth. My father did the same thing. Dad once told me, "When you were born, you were different from all the others. Something about you was special; I discovered this as I watched you grow up." He named me after the prophet, Samuel.

My brothers and I were all so different in our personalities, with our own beliefs and views. We didn't have the same gifts or abilities, and we were each unique in our own way. My father was a people person and wise enough to recognize the differences in our personalities, abilities, manners, and strengths; that required a deep degree of insight on his part.

※

As my siblings and I grew older, my dad told us that when his father, my Grandpa Nute Carter, was just thirteen years old, he had been snatched away from his family by slave owners. Grandpa's new owner's last name was Carter, and that is how our family got our name. It was hard for my father to talk about Grandpa Nute. Tears would come to Dad's eyes when he talked about how the slave owners had taken my grandfather away from his own parents, who were, of course, also slaves.

The more we learned about our grandfather, the more we understood why our father had always been so protective of us. My father always swore that we, his children, would never be servants to anyone as long as he was alive. We understood.

Even as kids, we felt the impact racism had on our father's life and our own lives.

Racism is still a global concern; it is systemic and controls the ways in which governments are run, even in the United States. Systemic racism is evidenced in the ongoing mass incarceration of black people within the criminal justice system, longer sentencing for blacks who commit the same crimes as whites, and the senseless shooting of unarmed black men and boys. Today my own daughters, who are female and black, "double minorities" as far as society is concerned, still face many of the same challenges in corporate America— lack of respect, unequal pay, etc.—that I faced back in the 1970s.

Simply put: things have not changed.

For the past four hundred years, black people in the United States of America have been forced into submission by (and to) white people. Within that period of time, we have been stripped of our culture, have seen our families separated and our children taken from their parents. We have seen our men castrated, and our people lynched. The lives of black people have been filled with abuse, violence, cruelty, and oppression, leaving deep psychological and emotional scars that last through the generations. But, through all of the oppression and crises, and despite the hardships, our people have survived to do great things.

Harriet Tubman, conductor of the Underground Railroad, risked her own life to lead a network of secret routes and help fugitive slaves escape to freedom.

Rosa Louise McCauley Parks, an activist in the Civil Rights Movement, played a pivotal role in the Montgomery bus boycott by not giving her seat to a white person.

Martin Luther King Jr., our dominant leader of the United States Civil Rights Movement, believed that nonviolent protests were the most effective weapon against a racist and unjust society. He gave his life for the cause, but he is alive with us in spirit.

There are many other unnamed black heroes who have done great things despite the obstacles against them, and there are many more who are doing great things today.

As I think of all these incredible black men and women, my question is: who or what inspired them to do those things when all odds were against them? I figure it had to be a supreme something within them. Personally, I believe that supreme something was the Spirit of the living God who instilled them with a divine compulsion to give so freely of their services to a community that was so deeply scarred.

Sadly, however, injustice leaves scars that never heal.

GRANDPA NUTE

It is almost unbearable to think of what life was like for black people in the 1800's South. By design, any unity or coherence was out of their grasp. Individuals were separated from their families, put on the auction block, and sold to the highest bidder to be given the names of their slave masters. Their sons and daughters were taken and sold as well. Slaves lived in a world of anguish, scorn, and savage bitterness. The brutality and inhumane treatment from our country's forefathers took such a psychological and emotional effect on my ancestors, it has lasted through the generations. When my father would talk about how Grandpa Nute was treated, I could feel Grandpa's pain as if it traveled through time.

Grandpa Nute was born into slavery in the early 1800s. Back then, black people worked without pay and were frequently beaten, and black women were often forced to have sexual relations with their owners. Whites were allowed to integrate with blacks, but it was a crime for blacks to integrate with whites. Slave owners regularly separated families by taking the wives and either keeping them for themselves, or selling them. They would also sell slave children to other slave owners as if they were cattle.

Grandpa Nute was only thirteen years old when he was torn away from his parents. He was too young to know or remember how his parents had been treated or what had happened to them. He had only the vivid memory of being taken from his family, of screaming for help, and of his parents' helplessness as they had no power or authority to rescue him from the slave traders. He'd had sisters and brothers as well, but he couldn't remember anything about them beyond their existence. All Grandpa was able to tell my father was how he, and all black people at the time, had been abused. It was more than my father could bear to hear.

My father first shared Grandpa Nute's story with me when I was fifteen years old; he thought I was mature enough then to hear it. He'd told my older brothers years before me, but beyond that, he seldom talked to us about Grandpa Nute's upbringing; Grandpa's story was too painful to mention.

The slave traders sold Grandpa Nute to Carter's Plantation, and that last name became his. His original name, now unknown to my family, was no longer mentioned; only the name "Carter." He was stripped of everything: his name, identity, religion, and culture. He was still just a child, alone and living in a strange land by himself with no one to talk to and no one to comfort him. He became a herdsman for his slave master and worked hard to care for the cattle. He did not have sufficient clothing or even shoes to wear, so when it got cold in the winter, he would make the cows get up from lying down. He would then place his feet on the ground where the cows had lain so he could warm his feet.

Conditions on the plantation were almost unlivable. Grandpa slept in a ramshackle barn where hay was his bed and feed sacks, his bed coverings. He ate scraps from his master's meals. He was impoverished, overworked, and mistreated. And he was alone; he had no companionship. Grandpa Nute wasn't allowed to talk to other slaves for fear they might try to plan an escape. He never did attempt to run away, knowing he would most likely be caught, beaten, and returned to the master's plantation.

There was a law at the time that anyone who gave food or shelter to a runaway slave would be fined and put in prison. Of course, the Underground Railroad was in full operation then, helping slaves to escape to freedom, but Grandpa was not aware of it. Even if he had been, he wouldn't have had the support to escape anyway. Still, despite the circumstances, Grandpa Nute was a man of great faith. He always knew he would be a free man one day.

In 1863, the Civil War ended, the Emancipation Proclamation was passed, and, just like that, Grandpa Nute was a free man. He was eighteen years old at the time. Having been a slave, he had no resources of his own and no formal education. It was like being born anew; he had to start from scratch. He considered trying to find his parents, but he had no way of knowing where they were. They had been sold as well, so he didn't even know their names.

Though he had no means of transportation, Grandpa was determined to make a life for himself. It must have taken great courage to overcome the odds that were stacked against him, but after becoming a free man, he stayed in Alabama in a little community in Butler County called Chapman. That's where he met and married my grandma, Mariah.

My grandmother was also a former slave, though I don't know much else about her. My father never spoke much of her; perhaps it was too grievous for him, though I don't really know his reason. But there in Alabama, Grandpa Nute and Grandma Mariah started their own family. They had seven strong boys: Morgan, Wiley, Ed, Aubrey (my father), Will, Martin, and Dave, and four lovely daughters: Mary, Heddie Bell, Mammie, and Lula Bell. I had the pleasure of meeting all of my father's brothers and sisters and would become close to each of them over the years.

Grandpa Nute regularly told his sons and daughters about his experiences as a slave, and the things he'd had to endure. Those were incredibly difficult and terrifying stories for them to hear, but he told them anyway. He wanted them to understand the times and the social conditions in which they were living so they could survive, like he had. He was frank about the violent racism of the time and the lynching of blacks for no reason. Grandpa told them the truth: slavery was a "cursed and wicked thing." He taught his children to never be a slave to any person, system, or religion, the same lesson my father would then pass down to my siblings and me.

Grandpa shared his experiences to teach his children how they could overcome any obstacle or barrier they might be faced with. He taught them the importance of sticking together and supporting each other, as he understood the importance and strength of having a large family. To Grandpa, a big, strong family represented power and protection from the forces of racism and slavery he had experienced all of his life. He instilled in his family a sense of compassion and care for one another; he showed them how to support each other by exhibiting respect and love. He knew that treating others with respect and love was the only way to find true liberation.

Though my grandfather died before I was born, I saw firsthand how much of a profound effect his past had on my father. Grandpa's lessons gave Dad the ability to perceive problems and the courage to confront and solve them. My father had the gift of discernment—he always knew who to hang around and who not to; and he was perceptive—he could always predict the outcomes of situations. In social activities, he taught us never to run with the crowd, but to be independent. And he told us never to call the police for help. Instead, we should run *from* them, because in those days, there were no laws to protect black people.

I sometimes feel sad that I never knew Grandpa Nute; I never had the chance to hear his voice or see his face, and I never knew what it felt like to be closely embraced in his arms. But through my father, I have a memory of him and, in a way, I know him. He is a part of me. We are a part of each other.

CHILDREN OF SLAVES

Truth is a hard pill to swallow. It can be difficult to accept the hard truths, even about ourselves. As humans, we like to blame others for our mistakes, actions, and wrongs. But Grandpa knew the only way to freedom was to accept the truth: the truth about himself, about the world, about life, and about his experiences as a slave. He shared this with his children so they'd know that freedom is not a guarantee; freedom must be a continued fight in this country.

Grandpa Nute's story had a deep and painful effect on my father. Each time Dad talked about his father, he would weep, thinking about how Grandpa had been treated. Dad was angry but determined to make life better for us.

Grandpa Nute raised his sons to be men who stood for justice and always fought against the forces of evil in the deep South. My father and his brothers were very close and had a lot of love and respect for each other. They were humanitarian people and looked out for others wherever they went. But they refused to be treated unjustly by anyone.

My father had listened and taken it to heart when Grandpa warned him to never start trouble, fights, or arguments, and to never take anything from anybody. Grandpa wanted his children to stand up for themselves. He taught them to always face crises, not to run from them. As a result, my father never ran from anything.

❦

As he grew up, my dad, Aubrey Carter, was a force to be reckoned with. He was equipped with a fundamental understanding of how the world's class system worked, and how society was able to deal with the racial tension and violence his family faced. He was a black man born in 1897 when there were no laws in place to protect black people. My father always said, "justice begins when and where injustice presents itself." He did not start trouble and he did not run from it, but he had the courage and back bone to face injustice—and resist it.

Dad told my siblings and me that when he was a young man, on his way home from work one day, a man had come up behind him and hit him in the head with a shovel, leaving him for dead. Dad was knocked unconscious and his skull was crushed, but thankfully, he came to and walked himself home. The fracture was so bad, a doctor put a steel plate in his head. Mind you, it was the early 1900s in Alabama, the deep South, where no medical facilities such as hospitals or urgent care were available. My father had at his disposal only a few local doctors' offices. But by the grace of God, there was someone with enough medical knowledge and skills to treat my father's injury and resulting illness, and though it took a long time for him to recover, he had no lasting brain damage as a result of his injuries.

My father knew the man who had attacked him, but just barely; the person was a black man and they were acquaintances. You see, my father was well-known. He was a handsome, single man at the time, and he got a lot of girls. A girl had taken a liking to my father, and this guy was jealous. Apparently, that was all the reason this man needed for attacking my father. Worst of all, there was nothing my father could do about it, at least, not right away.

As Dad regained his strength, he considered the insane deed that had been committed by a man he barely knew. My father had never once done or said anything to offend this man in any way. So, once my father had fully recovered, he began searching for the man who had almost ended his life.

It took months. Finally, Dad went to church one Sunday morning and saw the man standing outside, waiting to go in. He did not see my dad, but my dad sure saw him. Dad immediately turned around, went home, got his shotgun, and returned to the church. He waited until church services were over. When the man came out, my father was waiting for him. When he tried to run, my father shot and killed him right there in front of everybody.

There were no repercussions, no jail time. That's just how it was.

This all happened when my father was a young man, years before I was born, but I do remember when and how I first heard the story. You see, Ray had taught me how to cut hair, so I used to cut my dad's hair every week. Dad cared a lot about how he looked, and I would cut his hair by hand with a pair of clippers. One day, I was cutting his hair and I noticed the scar on his head, so I asked him about it. He was cool and calm as he explained to me what had happened. He wasn't angry anymore. Hearing him tell that story, I was proud of him for standing up for himself, though not to the extreme degree of murder. Still, it never changed the way I thought of my father. He'd acted out of retribution.

*

When we were young, my father would take my siblings and me to visit my aunts and uncles every two years, and they would visit us every other year, as well. All of my dad's brothers lived in central Florida with their families, just ninety miles from our house and near a little town out in the country called Century. Ninety miles may not sound like much by today's standards, but at that time, it was a long trip to take. Living in the South in the 1950s was not easy. Although we had our car by that time, money was tight, and we were not able to go on long trips in those times. We would only go when it was convenient for us to do so. Many times we simply could not afford the trip. It was a three-hour drive to Century, and for most of the journey, we'd travel on a narrow road with a speed limit of about forty miles per hour. Many of the other roads were unpaved, which slowed us down considerably. Making that trip was a big deal, so when we'd go to visit, everyone would get together.

One of my father's brothers, Will Carter, was a Baptist minister, the only one in the family. I remember him coming to our church in Alabama and running a revival. It was a great experience for us—and especially for me—to hear and see him. Uncle Will preached the gospel, but he also believed strongly in justice and fair treatment. He once killed another black man for trespassing on his property and endangering his family. The man had come to Uncle Will's house, walked up to the porch, and tried to force his way inside. The intruder was a known bully in the community and went for bad. My uncle had no other choice but to shoot to kill.

My father's oldest brother, Uncle Wiley, owned land, had a wonderful home, and owned a business selling syrup. He worked for himself. Uncle Wiley and his wife, Ella, had seventeen children, and he was a wonderful husband, father, and then grandfather until he was killed in 1963. He was close to a hundred years old at the time. Uncle Wiley had been about to receive an award for being the oldest citizen in town before he was killed. His killer was a white man who had wanted to borrow some of my uncle's syrup-making tools. My uncle told the man to use his own tools. After that, this man didn't want Wiley to win the award, so he shot him. My uncle had been on his way home and was alone when a group of men came up from behind and ambushed him.

According to John Paul Carter, Uncle Wiley's great, great, great grandson, the wife of the man who killed Wiley came to the house years later and confessed to Aunt Ella that her husband had been the killer. The woman's husband had passed away by then, and she'd kept his secret for years, afraid that she'd be killed too.

※

I also remember my father's youngest sister, Lula Bell. When Aunt Lula Bell was a young girl, having heard the story of her father's life of turmoil, stress, oppression, and despair, she became determined to make a better life for herself. Her mind was made up: she would leave the deep South where her father had been a slave; she would have none of that for her life. As such, she left the South at a young age and went to Washington, DC, in pursuit of a more productive life.

Because Lula Bell lived in Washington, DC, I never got a chance to meet her when I was a kid. Then, when I was twenty-two years old, I was in a singing group called The Soul Searchers. We had a concert in DC, and I went to Lula's house to meet her for the first time. She was sick and bedridden, but I spent the day talking with her and listening to her stories. She said I sounded so much like my father. Aunt Lula Bell told me about how she had gotten married and left home at a young age, and she hadn't been back since. I was so glad I got to meet her; I was the only one of my brothers and sisters who had that opportunity.

Aunt Lula Bell was a wealthy woman with no children. She had financial investments and stocks in oil, and when I met her, she told me she wanted me to have them. I couldn't accept her offer. It simply wasn't in my upbringing to take things from people. My parents had always taught us to give, give, give. At the time, I didn't realize she didn't have children and that she wanted to leave her investments to her family. After that, I stayed in touch with my aunt, but I never saw her again. To this day, I regret not taking the money.

Each of my aunts and uncles was affected by Grandpa Nute's story in his or her own way, and each one of them was kind and deeply compassionate. Through them I've learned that it's best to always be kind to people when you meet them; you don't know what they've been through or are going through.

My Mother's Family

I do not know the lineage of my Grandpa Nute and that side of the family, but I do know that my mother's great grandmother was born in Ethiopia and was taken to Haiti, where my mother's grandmother was born. From there, my mother's grandmother came to Alabama, where *my* grandmother, Emily Hamilton May, was born. The struggles and hardships of these women were not discussed, but I believe it had to have been a grievous journey for them. It was a hardship for all people of color in those days.

Unlike my father's family, my mother and her family were not descendants of slaves. When they moved to America, however, they were still seen in that light. This was a country that had enslaved people of African descent for hundreds of years. Suddenly, they found themselves in a place where they were thought of as "other" or "less than." Their "non-whiteness" made them victims here in the racist South.

❦

I am blessed to have known both of my grandparents on my mother's side: Grandpa Dunk May and Grandmom Emily Hamilton May. Grandpa Dunk was gentle, compassionate, and kind, with a way of saying things that did not offend but still got his point across. I never saw him get upset or angry; he was always calm. He always had something good to say, and he lived to be one hundred years old. I always wanted to be like Grandpa Dunk when I grew up. He was fun to be around, in control of himself, and in a world of his own.

Now, Grandmom Emily—she was a woman of good understanding. She had a beautiful countenance and was very intelligent. She had a meek way about her that demanded respect, but I remember laughing with her and having so much fun.

Grandpa Dunk and Grandmom Emily raised seven children—six girls and one son. All of them were good and respectful aunts and uncles to my siblings and me. They all set a pattern for the rest of us to follow as parents and later as grandparents.

As they got older, Grandpa and Grandmom would stay at each of their daughters' homes for two weeks, then go to another daughter's house to stay. We could not wait for our turn for them to visit us, because we enjoyed them so much. We had a fireplace in the living room of our house, and when they came to stay with us, we would all sit around the fireplace with Grandmom in the center and just listen to her talk. I can remember her sitting erect with perfect posture, telling us stories of the past. She never dwelled on the bad and negative, but only the good and positive things.

I remember once playing a game with Grandmom; I described an animal to her to see if she could name it. I said to her, "Grandmom, name this animal. He has a long tail with a long tongue. He has a long, skinny face with big eyes, and he looks sneaky. What is the name of that animal?" She paused, looked at me solemnly, but with a hint of wit, and said, "It's you!" We all began laughing. It lasted for a long time. Grandmom laughed so hard, she began to cry as she laughed. We had so much fun with her.

Grandpa Dunk smoked a pipe that gave off a sweet smell, and when he smoked it, we could smell it throughout the whole house. We loved to visit with him as well.

Nothing seemed to upset Grandpa and Grandmom, though we treated them with great respect. We never called them by their names, Dunk or Emily; we always called them Grandpa and Grandmom. We had the utmost respect for both of them, and we would not say anything disrespectful in their presence.

The house we rented and lived in at the time was one we'd moved to in 1951, when I was nine years old. It was a big house with five bedrooms. Houses in that area were named based on the landowner or a natural feature, like "Picken Rawls," a local landowner, or "Mayberry Gulley," where my family lived. The name "Mayberry Gulley" came from the huge, gaping hole in the ground that was down the road from the house. About eight or nine years ago, my wife, children, and I got a chance to visit Mayberry Gulley, and the house was still standing then. Years ago, my dad showed Willie and me where the Picken Rawls house had likely stood.

Two of the bedrooms had fireplaces, my father and mother's bedroom and the bedroom I shared with my brothers. The kitchen was large, with a long eating table that could sit thirteen. My mother's cooking stove was not electric; it was a wood-burning stove. I had hoped my father would buy that house since it was big enough to accommodate all eleven of us who lived there at the time, plus Grandpa and Grandmom when they came to visit, but as a sharecropper, he just rented homes in those days.

EARLY LIFE

Living in the country in rural Alabama had its advantages. I consider myself lucky to have grown up there, and think it is a good place to be from. I learned fast and grew up quickly. I had seen grown men who acted like children early on in my life, and I quickly learned ways of adapting to all different kinds of settings and environments. For me, childhood lasted until about eight years old. By ten or eleven years old, I could talk to people, young or old. After that, I could comprehend life, and I was an adult. I had wisdom. Wisdom is about how you conduct yourself; age has nothing to do with it.

As a boy growing up in Alabama, I was able to see nature in its completeness. I enjoyed watching each season pass—winter, spring, summer, and autumn—but spring was my favorite season. That time of year, there were trees in the back of the house that bloomed: pecan, peach, pear, and fig. You could see and hear the singing birds as they flew from limb to limb. My mother had a beautiful garden where she planted all kinds of vegetables: tomatoes, peas, turnips, and many others. The smell was delightful. Us kids were not allowed to pick any fruit or vegetable until it was fully ripe, but we were tempted.

My mother would harvest fruit in the summer to can for the winter. My parents did not go grocery shopping every week; most everything we needed came from the farm. My father had hogs and cows that he killed for meat, there were fruits and vegetables from the garden, and we had syrup from his sugarcane farm.

The "rolling store" would come to the house every two weeks. This was a store on wheels that carried all types of products: sugar, spices, flour, cooking oil, and other things. My parents bought just the products we didn't raise on the farm. There was also an ice truck that came every two weeks. We didn't own a refrigerator; we had an ice box. My father would buy fifty pounds of ice every two weeks to keep the food cool. The ice didn't cost a lot, otherwise we wouldn't have been able to afford it. It was probably less than a dollar.

Farming was a hard way to make a living. My dad and brothers, Eugene, AC, Raybon, and Huston, would work in the fields from sunup to sundown, five days a week. Saturday was a day for relaxation and doing small things around the house. Sunday was for church.

I was too young at that time to do farm work; my dad wouldn't let me and said I was too weak. I was glad, as farming was *not my thing*. My father planted cotton, corn, and peanuts as his three main crops. When I turned fifteen, I would help in the field, picking cotton, stacking peanuts, and pulling corn. By that point, farming had become fun and exciting, but only because it was my choice to do it. Of course, I also did the work since it was the right thing to do. Ray, being more of a farmer than myself, had started working on the farm at age eight. He was big and strong at that age, and my father knew he was strong enough to work.

Our parents taught us that we must work for what we have and not depend on others for the things we needed. They set a good example for us to follow and as I grew, I wanted to be like my father. He was wise, strong, and a protector of his family.

We did a lot of moving back then. We would stay somewhere for five years and then we would move. We didn't own our homes; that is how sharecroppers lived. If we'd had ownership, then we could have stayed. This made me dream of owning my own home someday. I wanted a home for my family when I grew up. We—me, my sisters, and my brothers—all hated farm work deep down, but it was the only way of making a living in rural Alabama.

Growing Up in the
Jim Crow South

When I was a little boy, back in the 1940s, we did not own a car or truck. Our only means of transportation was Dad's wagon, pulled by a couple of mules. Life was simple and plain. There wasn't really any rivalry of class, race, or gender in our community, because everyone lived in the same conditions. We were all farmers, poor people who worked and lived for the interest of our families. There were more white than black families in the community. Whites kept to themselves and blacks to themselves; segregation was the law in the South, but everyone knew each other. We all got along.

Although we were poor, we were raised with pride. Money did not dictate our lives. We were able to use what we had in simple and dignified ways. Nobody stole or took anything away from others. We worked for what we had and shared the fruits and vegetables we'd grown on the farm.

Still, growing up in the South during the pre-civil rights era in a sharecropping family of seventeen wasn't easy. There were no opportunities for upward movement. Whatever we were doing then was all we could ever hope to do. Jim Crow was still in effect, so we couldn't go to the white schools, like Rawls School, which was right down the road from our house. Instead, we rode a bus and had to go to the black school.

Everything was separate but *nothing* was equal. Designated areas for blacks were always in poor condition. We got used books from the white schools, and everything was labeled "black" or "white," including the water fountains. There were no blacks on the police force. The drive-in and indoor movie theaters were segregated; we had to park in the back of the drive-in, and at the theater, the white seating was downstairs, while the black seating was upstairs in the balcony. We even had all-black football teams and basketball teams.

Despite all this, at the time of my life, segregation did not matter to me; I knew who I was. My parents had taught me to have pride and self-respect.

♣

I remember one day in 1950 before we'd gotten our first car. My brother Raybon was riding one of my father's mules, named Jeff. Jeff was a male mule with a chestnut color. He was medium-sized with the characteristics of a horse; he could run fast, was full of energy, and was easy to ride. We rode our mules "Indian Style" (bareback), as we couldn't afford saddles at that time.

Raybon was on his way home from the grocery store with sugar and cooking oil that my parents had told him to get. As he rode, he passed one of our neighbors who was riding a bicycle. The boy's name was Douglas Taylor, and he was a white boy, the same age as Ray. When Douglas saw Ray riding past, he shouted "Nigger, nigger, nigger!" and then continued on his way. Ray was surprised. He and Douglas knew each other and were even friends.

Raybon came home and told my father the story. My father looked stern, but didn't seem particularly angry. He gathered all five of us boys and took us to Douglas Taylor's house. When Mr. Taylor came outside, Dad said, "Your son called my son a nigger." His voice was very matter-of-fact.

Mr. Taylor turned red and clenched his fists. He called Douglas out of the house right away and, very seriously but without raising his voice, asked Douglas if he'd said that word to Ray. Douglas said, "Yes." When Mr. Taylor heard his son's response, he gave Douglas a whopping in front of all of us and told him it was wrong what he had done. He whopped him real good.

Before we left, Mr. Taylor apologized to my father for what his son had said to Ray. My father, as calm as could be, said, "It's all right; it's done," and we went home.

On the way home, Raybon started to laugh at the way Douglas had been beaten in front of us; he thought it was funny. Immediately, my father stopped the wagon and glared at Raybon. He said, "If you laugh again, I will give you the same whopping Douglas got." Raybon never laughed about it again. From then on, Douglas and Ray were friends again and rode their bikes as usual. I was a young boy at that time, eight years old, but it was a moment I never forgot.

That was the first time I had ever heard the "N-word." I didn't know what it meant, because I had never heard it used in the family, and of course, didn't understand its roots. But even as a child, I knew it was a word meant to degrade someone's character. My father had been wise enough to confront that crisis by responding to it in an effective and appropriate way. He was cool and kept everybody calm. We were taught by our parents to have a good level of self-respect and to discern what was just and right.

Now that I'm an adult, I know we must always confront injustice and racism. People are not born racist, they are taught by their parents and their peers. Still, racism controls many things in this country: our economy, labor, education, and even justice.

Sometime that same year, my brothers and I were playing in a field near the house. Two or three young white girls approached Ray. Ray had always been tall, dark, and handsome, with a head full of hair. The girls were gushing and giggling, and it was clear they admired him. Fortunately, my father saw what was going on and ordered Ray to get in the house. Dad understood the dangers of black boys even looking at white girls, let alone interacting with them, and Ray knew he was in trouble. In the 1950s, in segregated states, there was a law that black men couldn't even look at white women. The law was called "reckless eyeballing" and the punishment was severe—sometimes even death. I was just a child, but I knew what my father was doing when he called for Raybon. He was protecting him from those white girls. He was protecting him from becoming a victim. My father was protecting his son.

CHILDHOOD: THE DARK AND THE LIGHT

I remember when we got our first car. I was almost nine, and my brothers Huston and Raybon were thirteen and fourteen, respectively, when they bought it. They had planted cotton on three acres of land owned by Mr. Picken Rawls, who the local white school had been named for. They cultivated the land, planted and picked the cotton, and then sold it at the gin mill. Eventually, they made enough money to buy the first car for our family. It was an exciting time for all of us to make the shift from a mule and wagon to a car.

That first car was a 1940 Plymouth, black with four doors, for which Huston and Raybon paid $120. I can remember everything about it—its new smell and how it looked. With it, we gained a sense of freedom. We were no longer limited by distance when we traveled, nor were we restricted by the weather; we could go as we pleased. I felt proud. Our family had gone from a laughing stock to elite. We would take our new car to the grocery store or to church, with my mother in the front middle seat, my dad in the passenger seat, and us kids in the back. One of my brothers usually drove. As young teenagers, Raybon and Huston had had the wisdom to understand what was needed for the family. They took the initiative and used their new incomes to make life better for all of us.

Soon after, we drove our car to Century, Florida. As I mentioned earlier, Century was about ninety miles from our home, and my father had six brothers who lived there. Once we got our car, we loved to go visit our family there. A few of us Carters would always have to stay home as we were such a large family, but eight of us would pack into the car—three in the front and five in the back seat. We were average-sized kids and were able to all fit with comfort.

I remember our first trip to Florida. It was an adventure to me, even the ride itself: going through little towns; looking at the stores and homes; stopping at railroad tracks to wait for the train to pass, its wheels squeaking as it rolled by. It was all a new experience for me, and when we finally got to Florida, I was so excited to meet my uncles for the first time.

Later, I learned how to drive that car. Ray and Huston had always driven me everywhere, and I would watch them drive. I had studied so carefully how they held the steering wheel and shifted gears that I could already drive at eleven years old. I loved to drive around with my big brothers. I would sit at the front edge of the seat so I could reach the pedals, and someone would always ride with me to make sure I was safe. Even at such a young age, I was already becoming an adult.

※

1956 was a formative year for me. I turned fourteen years old that year, and was settling firmly into being a man. Although most people think manhood begins at a later age, I felt and still feel that my childhood was short; I grew up fast. It was at that time I began experiencing what would become a common crisis in my life. Now, everyone will face a crisis at some point in their lives, but even at fourteen, I knew things never stayed the same, no matter how bad they were; conditions could and would always get better.

In those days, I was in charge whenever my father was not home. My brothers were all living in Niagara Falls, New York by that point, along with two of my sisters, Dixie Lee and Mammie Paul. As the designated man of the house, I felt desperate and lonely. Although I was living at home with my sisters and my father, there was a missing piece, a disconnection in my life. My mother was sick with a blood disorder and living in a nursing home about forty miles away, near Troy, Alabama. Our small town lacked the resources to provide adequate treatment for her condition.

I had suddenly found myself with more responsibility than most fourteen-year-olds could even dream of. Part of that meant protecting my sisters while our father was away, working. I remember one evening in particular when two men came to see Operee and Aubrey Lee. My sisters were older than me, and even though they had watched over me when I was a child, I was still in charge of protecting them. Operee was in her twenties and Aubrey Lee was in her thirties. Both of them were separated from their husbands, and both of the men visiting them were married.

It was around 7:00 p.m. when I found the four of them sitting in the living room. It made me uncomfortable to see my two still-married sisters, even if they were separated, spending time with these two married men after dark. As the man of the house, I made a decision to protect my father's house and my sisters' dignity. I told the two men it was about time for them to leave. I remember coming back thirty minutes later, only to find them still there. I left the room again, and came back shortly with my father's shot gun. Once they saw the gun, they got up and ran out of the house. They never came back. They had not shown respect for me, or for my father's house, so I ran them out.

Growing up, I always loved and admired my brothers for their courageousness. Eugene and AC would always work in the woods, cutting timber with my father, while Raybon and Huston worked in the fields, plowing the land with two of our mules, Mutt and Kate. Most evenings, after their hard day's work, they would go out on the front porch, and I would join them. Surrounded by my brothers, I always felt protected, empowered by their presence. They were my big brothers, and they referred to me as their little baby brother. Everywhere they went, they would take me along with them.

AC and Raybon would sometimes take me with them on their dates. I recall one specific night when Raybon took me to see a lady friend of his. It was dark and in the early parts of the night, and when we got to her house, Ray told me to stay in the car, instructing me to lock the doors and not let anyone in. I waited and waited and waited, and finally, he returned to the car. "That was a long prayer," I said, as he climbed into the driver's seat. Ray just laughed and we went home.

Little did I know at that time, but my brothers were teaching me how to function on a level of emotional and psychological maturity. They nurtured me by protecting me and teaching me things they knew. Their experience and support made me the man I am today.

❦

Another vivid memory, though of a very different kind, comes from that same year. We lived in the countryside, where the nights were so dark you couldn't see your hands in front of your face. Lightning bugs would fly around, and every few seconds, they'd be somewhere else, flashing in a different place than before. I would lie in bed and just watch the bugs light up the dark night, going wherever they wanted to. I would watch them disappear in the distance, into the darkness, my eyes transfixed on what I will always remember to be truly amazing. It was a transformative sight. All of the difficulties I had faced, and would face, seemed to fade away as I watched those lightning bugs.

My mother was still in the nursing home, and I felt sad and empty in her absence. I was left alone with five of my sisters, and instructed to keep the home functioning while my father worked to provide for the family. Money was tight and we did not always have the resources we needed.

Lying in bed, watching the lightning bugs flying around suddenly made me look at my situation in a different way. I saw the night as the hardships, disappointments, distress, and sadness in life, but I saw the lightning bugs as hope, faith, and confidence that there is light in the darkness if you keep your faith.

When you think about it, we are all lights. In Matthew 5:14-16 (King James Version), Jesus said, "Ye are the light of the world. A city that is set on a hill cannot be hid. Neither do men light a candle and put it under a bushel, but on a candlestick; and it giveth light unto all that are in the house. Let your light so shine before men, that they may see your good works, and glorify your Father which is in Heaven."

Through my experiences and upbringing, I was given the ability to see my own light, to become my own man, and to do things in what I believed was God's way.

Dealing with my mother's illness when I was just fourteen was a dark time, as was her death when I was seventeen. But by then I knew to depend on my faith; it wasn't the first time faith had pulled me from the darkness and into the light. One particularly profound moment of darkness had occurred when I was just nine.

When I turned nine, I experienced my first moment of true darkness after AC gave me my first rifle. It was an old rifle that had been made in the 1800s. It broke down like a shot gun and used 22-caliber shells. I was thrilled to have a gun of my own for the first time, and I thanked him. AC explained to me that the gun was to be used for pleasure. He said to me, "I just want you to have this gun. Be careful, don't hurt yourself and nobody else." I remembered feeling empowered. I could protect myself, even if my brothers were not around.

One afternoon, I decided to go hunting by myself. I wasn't looking for any special game in particular; I was looking for anything to shoot at. I was moved and thrilled to have a gun to hunt with. It was a beautiful day, so I loaded my gun, and into the woods I went. The weather was clear, and I could see the birds flying and the squirrels in the trees. I was not a hunter like my father or my brother Huston. Huston was an excellent marksman. He could strike a match with a rifle twenty yards away. I was just having fun. I took a few shots at birds and missed; I shot at a couple of rabbits and missed. And after a short while, all of the cartridges were used up.

On my way home, I walked along a narrow trail next to the field where my father was farming. I looked down, and there was a 22-caliber cartridge just lying there on the ground. It was the exact size for my rifle. I picked it up and wiped the dirt off. It must have been on the ground for a long time as it was covered with dirt.

After a moment, I loaded the cartridge into my gun and pulled the trigger. Instead of firing, however, the gun just clicked. I pulled the trigger and clicked it several more times, but it would not fire. Then I did something extremely dangerous. I put the gun to my head and pulled the trigger. Thank God, the cartridge was a dud.

As a child, I did not understand what could have been the consequences … not until later anyway. I just put the rifle on my shoulder and headed for home. As I was walking home, I looked up and saw a flock of birds flying south. Instinctively, I took the gun and aimed at the birds. I pulled the trigger and the gun fired. Panic hit me like a bolt of lightning. Instantly, I thought of my parents and how they would have felt about losing their youngest son. I thought of my whole family. I was shocked to the core of my heart.

I threw down the gun and ran home. I never told anyone what had happened. I thought it would have been too stressful for them to bear.

After that shell-shocking experience, I changed. I began to more deeply appreciate the gift of life and the fact that we live not for ourselves but for others. We are all connected, like a body—what affects one part affects the whole body. My whole family would have been socially, psychologically, mentally, and emotionally devastated if that gun had fired. It would have left them in a horrible state of mind for the rest of their lives.

I was sixty-five years old when I shared the story with my wife and daughters. Keeping this moment to myself through all those years, a moment upon which I would reflect from time to time, I realized God had kept me for His purposes. In an instant, our lives can be altered, and even terminated, over something trivial. I promised myself I would always think and never be careless over anything again. That was a turning point. I looked at life on a higher level after that, and I became spiritually aware. Now I believe things happen for a reason. And I believe God intervened that day; He stopped the bullet from firing to show me He was with me and had something for me to do.

What I remember most from my childhood is my family, specifically my mother and father, and how they kept us together as a strong family, equipping us to become men and women able to meet the challenges of the future and make a better life for the generations to come. They taught us how to be leaders, not followers. They invested their all in us so we could go forward in liberty and freedom.

As I matured, I applied to my life the lessons they taught me—to have great respect for myself and for others; to never be afraid to speak out on things that are unjust; to always approach things in an appropriate way; to remember the importance of good character, as it would follow me throughout my entire life; and to know I am in control of and responsible for my own destiny. I began to focus not just on the things I liked to do and the places I wanted to go, but on my purpose in life.

Now when I look back to when I was a young man, when all I had to worry about was having fun and making people laugh, I see that life is a circle and we are all a part of it. All of us face the same issues: sickness, stress, failure, success, and even death. Life does not discriminate like people do; it is a gift for all.

Grandpa Nute was a slave with a will to be free; he was not enslaved by his mind, but by his surroundings and conditions. Those were dark, evil times in which he lived. He kept the faith, though, believing that someday he would be a free man. In 1864, the Emancipation Proclamation passed. Then the real fight was on; Grandpa was liberated from slavery, but he had to fight into his new life. Liberty was a radical change from his old life of fear and bondage, and he'd find in this new world that he wasn't prepared to *live*. Still, he was determined to make a life for himself as a free man.

To this day, when I face a crisis in my life, I think of my Grandpa Nute's story, his enslavement, the cruel treatment he faced, and his faith and determination to be free despite all of it. His memory gives me hope that I can overcome any obstacle I face.

Young Adulthood— Niagara Falls, The Soul Searchers, and My Sweetheart

As I look back on my childhood, I am glad I was raised in the country, on a farm, where life was simple. The country was where I learned about the important things in life, like having a two-parent family with the care and love of a mother, the protection of a father, and guidance from both of them. I thank God for my parents, and for my upbringing. Their teaching and instruction equipped me to be the man I am today. Because of them, I am emotionally strong and capable of functioning in this society. My parents taught us kids to have a high level of self-respect and emphasized the importance of character.

Growing up in the country, I observed the cultivation of the fields, the planting of the crops, and the gathering of the harvest. These observations taught me how to wait, watch, and learn the process of growing. It was this slow learning process that crystallized my understanding of the human condition and our behavior. I learned that progress does happen, but it takes time. The country was beautiful and had its lessons, but ultimately we were in the deep South, in the state of Alabama, with its unjust laws and racist behaviors toward non-white people.

So, when I became a young man, it was time for me to go. You see, Alabama is a good place to be from. But after a while, you learn there's a boiling point. You learn. You *learn*. It's a good place to be from—not to be, but to be from.

I left Alabama in 1960, when I was seventeen years old. I was nearly a legal adult then, though I had already felt like a man for many years at that point. My mother had recently passed away, and now I *needed* to be a man. After Mom's funeral, Ray asked me to come to Niagara Falls. He was settled there, and he said that Niagara Falls was where all the factory jobs were starting to be. Ray had left Alabama for Niagara Falls when he was nineteen, and the only time he ever came back home to Alabama was for my mother's funeral. Once he left Alabama, he refused to go anywhere south of the Mason-Dixon line; he simply did not want to put up with the racism in the South anymore. He had settled in Niagara Falls for the jobs, and because that's where Dixie and Mammie Paul had already been living for about ten years. My siblings seemed to love it there, so I figured, "Why not?" Now, all these years later, Ray still refuses to leave the Niagara Falls area. He's always been stubborn and conservative, both with his cars—which he would keep for twenty or so years—and with leaving the comfort of his now home.

When I moved to Niagara Falls, I had never told my father I was leaving, so after settling there for a time, I returned to Alabama again in the summer of 1962 to see him. When I arrived back in Alabama, I realized how much things had changed in such a short time. My father had married a woman we called Miss Polly. I don't know when or how they met each other. I didn't know anything about her, really, at least not before they were married. I think my father needed companionship in his life, and I can fully understand his making that choice for himself. After my mother died, my desire was to make a better life for myself and my family, so I supported my father in his decision.

Operee and Aubrey also still lived in Alabama, and they had their own places, right next door to each other, where they lived with their children. I stayed with them that summer.

When summer was over, I went back to Niagara Falls. As soon as I got back to my new city, I told Raybon and Huston about the conditions my sisters were living in, with no men at home to protect them. Ray and Huston immediately began making plans for our sisters to move up to Niagara Falls to make better lives for their families. So, later that same year, Operee and her three boys, Leo, Thurman, and Curry, along with Aubrey and her two children, Delores and David, all joined us in Niagara Falls.

Raybon owned a home in which he rented out several apartments, so Operee and her sons lived there until she found her own place. Huston also owned his own home, and a building with apartments in it, so Aubrey Lee stayed in one of Huston's apartments with her kids.

Margaret, the youngest of my sisters, had stayed in Alabama, living with my father. However, two years later, she also came to Niagara Falls to join the rest of us. At one point in time, there were eleven of us Carter siblings all living there at the same time. Edna Jean was married at that point, and she still lived in Alabama with her husband, Early Gamble, and their two children, Rose and Greg, in a little town called Andalusia. They, too, would eventually move to Niagara Falls.

Two years later, in 1964, I joined a traveling singing group called The Soul Searchers. I was twenty-one years old at the time. The group's name was so fitting because those two years of traveling and singing, of being away from family and home, gave me the chance to grow mentally and spiritually, as I began to recognize the kinds of challenges I would face in life.

One time, our group was traveling through the state of Louisiana. We were on our way to a little city called Lafayette when our car broke down; it just stopped running, and we were about seventy miles from our destination. We were in the deep South, and now here we were: four black men on the side of the road—stranded. There were no gas stations and no telephone booths around. After a few minutes, a car pulled up behind us, and a man got out of the car to see what was wrong. He was a white man. We explained how our car had just stopped running and that we were a gospel singing group on our way to Lafayette for a singing engagement. To our surprise, the man offered to drive another group member and me the remaining seventy miles to our destination. And he didn't charge us a penny. The other two stayed behind, as the gentleman's car was not large enough to take all of us, and somebody needed to stay with our car. We sent help for our friends.

When we had reached our destination, the man said to us, "I want you to know that there are some good white folks in the South." I thought to myself, *God has good people everywhere, angels of all colors and creeds to help those in their time of need.* We tried to pay him, but he refused to accept our offer. He never told us his name and did not ask us for our names, but just went on his way. From that day forward, we referred to him as "the angel."

Truly, love knows no color.

By 1966, I had performed for thousands of people and made records for a recording company, "Peacock Records," out of Houston, Texas. The Soul Searchers released hit songs like "Lord, You Been Good to Me," "Come and Go to That Land," and "The Old Account." One of my dreams when I was a boy had been to sing, travel, and make records, and I was satisfied with my accomplishments. However, after two years on the road, I'd had enough of traveling from city to city and state to state, and I felt it was my time to head back home.

It just so happened that our last singing engagement was in Andalusia, Alabama, five miles from my father's home in a little town called Gantt. It was great to see him. We hadn't kept in touch, didn't talk or write letters, but I still knew where he lived. My group spent three days with him and Miss Polly. They treated us so well, and we ate like kings.

The guys were excited to meet my dad; they could see the resemblance in the way we walked and the way we talked. I always knew I had many of my father's mannerisms; to this day, my sisters often tell me I act just like "Poppa."

Before we left my father's home, Dad told me he didn't think singing would be a successful career path for me. He wanted to see me settle down, get a job, and start a life. So, he was happy when I told him I was on my way back to Niagara Falls to do just that. I knew he was glad when I told him, because he gave me a nod with his head—Dad's way of saying, "Okay."

I decided to close that chapter of my life, and ended it on a high note, before heading back home to Niagara Falls, New York, to start a new chapter. I still kept in touch with the group for years afterward and attended one of their shows in Buffalo. I was happy for them, but I had no desire to travel again. The guys told me they'd sung with Michael Jackson and the Jackson Five in Chicago, where they performed on a TV program and made more money in one week than they usually made in a year.

In July of that same year, I made it back home to Niagara Falls. I was glad to be home, excited to see my girlfriend, Monica, and happy to see my brothers and sisters who had also settled there. I had so much fun with each one of them and loved them all greatly.

Around that time, I began looking for a job to earn some real money the way my father had advised me to. This is what I had originally planned to do when I had first moved to Niagara Falls four years prior, and I was finally back on track. I put in an application at a chemical manufacturing company named Carbo, and one week later, they called me for an interview. I got the job. I worked as a laborer, which entailed operating a regrading machine that separated various materials. The job provided steady income with health benefits and retirement, as well. After working there only three months, I bought a new 1967 Mustang. It was red, and I was so proud of that car. It was the first car I'd ever bought, and I paid $2,700—including tax. It was beautiful.

Knowledge of economics is important in all areas of life. Without money, life is deplorable and you are unable to meet basic needs. I learned from an early age the significance and importance of having money. I remember times when my parents could not afford to buy things we needed—be it a home, car, land; it was all about economics. My parents simply did not have the money. Everything in this world revolves around money, and at the beginning of 1967, I was glad to finally have some.

I was determined to make a better life for myself, financially and spiritually. I wanted a home of my own and a family, and I wanted to do it *my way*. So, after getting a job and a car and beginning to save some money, I took the next step in my life.

❧

Monica was my sweetheart, my love who had waited for me while I traveled the country and sang. It was unusual the way I had met Monica. It was an afternoon in March, 1964, around 3:15 p.m. I was cutting hair at my good friend, Roy Miller's house in Niagara Falls. Outside, I heard voices—laughter and talking—a group of girls on their way home from school.

When I looked to see who they were, they had already passed the house, and the only thing I could see were their backs. But there was one who got my attention: Monica. Her features were conspicuous. She had, and still has, beautiful bow legs that knocked me out. I didn't know who she was, her name, or where she lived, but I had to meet her.

As it turned out, I had a friend, named Sarah Baxter, who knew Monica. I asked Sarah to bring her to the Boys' Club where I was working. Three days later, Sarah brought Monica to meet me, and I was not disappointed when I saw her. She was a very attractive young woman. I asked for her phone number, and she was swift about writing it down for me.

One week later, I took Monica to the movies. I don't remember which movie we saw; it didn't matter because my attention was on her. We dated for two weeks before I thought to ask her about her age.

She replied, "Sixteen."

Oh, Lawd! I thought.

I was already twenty-one! Fortunately, however, I looked younger than my age. So, soon after, I went to her father, Mr. Herman Lane, and asked him for permission to date his daughter. I knew if I approached him in a respectful manner that I would be granted my wish.

I said, "Sir, I really like Monica, and she really likes me."

Thankfully, he said "yes," and I was granted the privilege of dating the beautiful Monica Lane. From that point forward, she became my lady and she has been for over fifty-two years now.

For the next two years, while I toured with The Soul Searchers, Monica had the patience to wait for me to come home—and I'm so glad she did. Not long after I moved back to Niagara Falls, I asked permission from Monica's mother, Mary Lane, to marry her. I remember so vividly, Mary smiled and said to me, "She is yours already, and always has been yours."

Shortly after, Monica and I took my red Mustang out to look for an engagement ring. I felt so proud, and she looked so beautiful and charming, as she always did. We went to a jewelry store, and after looking at rings for two hours, she finally found the one she wanted. Of course, I immediately bought it for her. We left, engaged and excited about making wedding plans.

Marrying my beautiful wife, Monica, was the best thing that ever happened to me. It made me feel complete. And I never forgot what Mary had told me; Monica had always been mine and always would be. Those words were a teaching I would embrace forever. This was a new chapter in my life, an unknown venture, and I began to settle down gradually as I learned how to be a good husband to my new wife. It wasn't simple, and in fact, I'm still learning, because the ways of women are unknown.

Marriage is not easy. You see her and she sees you. Each partner in the marriage brings baggage into a relationship that they are unaware of—their faults, habits, their particular ways of doing things that may still need to be refined and worked out. Both people must have an attitude of submission. It requires time and patience to learn and to submit willingly to each other. You must learn to solve problems together, and that can only happen with one another's input. Marriage is a daily process in which communication is a must. It requires patience, forgiveness, an understanding heart, and most importantly, a give-and-take relationship. All of these things lead to oneness.

Before our wedding, Monica and I started looking for an apartment, though we quickly discovered it was hard to find a place to live. It was 1967, and white people did not like to rent to blacks. Even though integration was the law, segregation was the reality. We searched for two weeks, and finally I was introduced to a man who was looking for someone to rent a complex with two apartments. So, I rented the whole complex. The landlord had wanted to sell the complex to me for $13,000, but no bank would give me a loan. I had gone to three banks for a mortgage loan and was turned down every time. Fortunately, both apartments had been kept up well, and the building was in a nice location one mile from the US/Canadian border in downtown Niagara Falls. Monica and I decided we'd live in the upstairs apartment, and we wound up subleasing the downstairs apartment to a white couple. It was great to feel like we were in charge; they paid their rent to *us*.

Monica and I spent hours cleaning that apartment, and when we finished, it looked brand new. We bought our furniture and got the apartment ready to move in after our wedding. We got married on a Saturday, April 22, 1967, and I went back to work the following Monday without taking a honeymoon; I was focused on money.

After they had lived in the apartment for two months, the people downstairs moved out. So, Operee and her three sons moved out of Ray's apartment, and we rented the space to her. She was very happy, and so was I. I had always been taught that family members should look out for each other and that black people, in particular, should help each other whenever they were in a position to do so. I was so glad to be able to help Operee. She had previously moved out of Raybon's house and into a different apartment, so she was happy to be living in our new house with family once again.

We didn't have any neighbors living next door, and it was quiet and peaceful. There was a gas station across the street and a small playground behind the house, with a tall fence that ran between the house and playground. Our parents had taught us to never forget where we came from, and I was so grateful for this new foray into renting a home. It presented an excellent opportunity for me to experience leadership on a new level. It also gave me the courage to find growth in situations of conflict.

It was a good place to live.

When our first child, Marilyn, was born, I took off from work to be there with my wife. Our baby was so beautiful, and I was so proud to be a father. I'll admit I had wanted a boy, but the One above knew best. When we returned home from the hospital, I held Marilyn and talked softly to her about how beautiful she was. My mind went back to when I was younger and how wonderful kind words had made me feel, and I realized those words had given me confidence. I continued to use those principles with Marilyn when she was young, always building her up with positive words. And, of course, having fun was a big part of our family life. Laughter is a powerful gift to share.

I felt like an adequate father, having drawn from childhood experiences. Growing up, I'd had the opportunity to develop and maximize a high level of maturity—emotionally, physically, mentally, and socially. I'd learned that parenting in our society required an understanding of correct behavior and discipline to help children achieve their ultimate goals.

In the early spring of 1968, after having worked for almost two years without a break, I was given two weeks of vacation time from the company, so my family and I made plans to visit my father in Alabama. I was excited for my dad to meet my family. My father did not know I had gotten married or that I had a daughter, and it was important to me that we reconnect after such monumental life events. After all, I had been taught by the very same man to never forget where I'd come from.

However, just two days before our departure, on April 4, 1968, the Reverend Martin Luther King Jr. was assassinated in Memphis, Tennessee. His death sent shockwaves around the world, and at the time, it seemed like the whole world stood still. People all over the country were stunned and confused. All throughout the South, there was fighting and rioting, and it was a dangerous place to be, so I felt compelled to cancel our vacation; I did not want to put my family at risk. I thought many days and nights about the tragedy after it happened, and the thought I returned to the most was: if one vicious act could have such a negative effect on our nation, what kind of effect might a positive act have? Wouldn't such an act have an equally but oppositely profound effect on humanity? It's amazing, how one person's act can have a transcendent effect on a generation of people, whether good or bad.

MAKING A BETTER LIFE

Our vacation having been postponed, I returned back to work. In 1969, there were more than three thousand employees working for Carbo, with many divisions, such as Boron, Armour (they made army vests for the government), and Electro Mineral (a division that manufactured products used to make sandpaper and other similar products). I worked for the Electro Mineral division.

My fellow employees came from different backgrounds and different walks of life. They were just regular people, and most of them were uneducated. Even the supervisors did not have degrees; they had obtained their positions based on who they knew in the company. I also noticed how most of the people working there were not content with their jobs. My coworkers would always talk about how many years they had been working and when they could retire. They did not enjoy where they were, at all. I felt their struggle, but I was glad to work there and make money for my family. By doing so, I was increasing my economic status, so I was grateful for the opportunity. I was a sifter operator, which required completing the correct setups, and understanding the nature and density of the products being sifted. My dedication to the job made me a productive employee.

At one point, the company had to lay off some of its employees for a short period of time, starting with those with the least seniority. There were plenty of employees who had more seniority than I had, so I was worried. Fortunately, the superintendent, Bill House, came to me privately and said, "There is going to be a lay off, but you won't be part of it." He added that he'd spoken to the top management and told them that he needed me there. He appreciated my skills and knowledge of the job, and thanked me for my wisdom. In return, I thanked Bill and told him I'd keep a low profile.

Before I started that position, I had been trained by Ding Smith, who had worked in the same role for over thirty years. Ding had become an expert, highly skilled in chemical sifting. He taught me all the tricks and trades of the job. Being a dedicated trainee, I bought a notebook and recorded all the information he taught me: the different setups for each of the products we used; when to vary speed control based on weather conditions (cold, hot, or damp); and how to distinguish the density of the products. Thanks to his training, and my experience, I became skillful at the job.

After some time, it became obvious that the white men in the company had a negative view of black people in positions of high authority such as supervisors, union stewards, or any other leadership positions. I then understood why there were no blacks in leadership positions. Black employees were elevator operators, sweeper operators, machine operators, or workers in the laboratory where the products were tested and analyzed, but there were no black foremen, electricians, or maintenance workers—only laborers.

As a black man, I saw this as racism, a system that prevented blacks from achieving high-level positions. In Alabama, racism had been the norm, a pattern that we lived by. Segregation was the law. Blacks went to black schools, blacks had to ride in the back of the bus, and there were even separate black and white water fountains. It was a pattern that existed throughout the South. When I came north, I discovered racism existed there too, but just in a different form. Racism was a worldwide epidemic, not just an isolated issue.

At that time, my main concern was to secure my position within the company by being a quality craftsman at work. Still, I began to think of how I could make things better, both for me and for my coworkers. As usual, I started with humor. I'd playfully encourage my coworkers by reminding them of the things they were good at, the gifts they possessed, and the knowledge they'd obtained from working for the company for so many years. After a while, some people seemed to take more of an interest in their work. The atmosphere was more pleasant, and for once, I started looking forward to going to work so I could talk to my friends. I began to enjoy each day and have fun, and, because I was so happy with myself, it rubbed off on my coworkers as well.

After a while, the people in management came to find out I could sing and play the guitar. So, Bill House asked me to be in charge of the entertainment committee for the company Christmas party. I gladly accepted. I formed a committee with three other men who worked at the company; two of us played guitar, and we all sang. The other men in the group included Bill, who was Scottish, had a thick accent, and was a talker; Red Hagel, a big, red-headed ladies' man; the other guitar player; and myself. We started rehearsing about a month before the Christmas party. We met one day each week, and it was great, because I got to meet new people, use my gifts, and develop my leadership skills. Nobody was ever late for practice, because we all loved to sing.

Funny, we never intended to become a formal singing group but had created the group for the purpose of getting three or four people to entertain the crowd at the Christmas party. After the singing group was formed, there were other men who wanted to join, but we kept it small.

When the Christmas party rolled around, it turned out my wife and I were the only black people who showed up. We still had a great time, though. My newly-formed band sang a few Christmas songs, and we even had people from the audience come up and sing. It went very well. After the party, Bill House asked me to get other black people to come the next year. I was heartened. And at the next year's Christmas party, six more people of color attended. It was always a fun and entertaining occasion, and all of us had a good time.

Carbo employed over three thousand people, and if you were good at playing sports, you were more likely to get a job there. The company had basketball, softball, and bowling teams. Our teams would play against teams from other companies. The year I played basketball, we lost the championship by one point. I was certain the coach who had showed racial favoritism to another player had contributed to our loss, and when they asked me to play again, I refused. I hate favoritism.

It was eight years later when the company needed someone to coach the basketball team—someone who could command respect, someone who was fair, and who could help them win a championship. They sent a friend of mine, John Mixon, to ask me to coach the team. I said I wasn't interested, but he pleaded, so I finally said, "yes."

I remember our first practice; twenty-eight men showed up to try out. *Woah, woah, woah,* I thought. I didn't want to cut anyone, so I asked everyone to sit down. I told them everyone would have a chance to play at some point, and no one would be a bench warmer. I also said I would try not to show favoritism toward any player, yet if we made it to the finals, *then* I would play the best players. Bingo! We ended up winning the championship that year.

We had a good basketball team—three of the players had played college ball and were extremely talented. It was a well-balanced team, with both black and white players. Everyone wanted to play. I was fair but firm with everyone, and they respected me because I treated every player the same.

I remember one game in which I started four white players and one black player. F. Carter, a black player on the team, complained to his teammates that I was showing favoritism toward the white players. He was a good player; he'd even had a tryout with the Buffalo Braves, a former professional basketball franchise. When I heard Carter say this, I stood up and told him, in front of the whole team, that if he didn't like what I was doing, he could leave. After that, I had no more trouble from him. Being a good leader is not about being popular; it's about standing up for what's right at the time and not allowing discrimination in the form of favoritism to exist. It's about helping a team to work together as a unit.

I coached that team for eight years, and we won five championships. Every player on the team played in every game, and they all knew they were a part of the team. No one sat on the bench, and I gained their respect as a leader. They all really wanted to win. But winning in sports is a difficult task, especially winning a championship. There are many variations to consider in a game—the skills of various players and matchups of various teams—and luck plays a big part in winning.

I remember we were playing a company called Olen in the championship one year. It was a *tough* game, and the bleachers were full of fans from both teams. With five minutes left in the game, we were down by eight points, and I called a time out and changed the lineup.

Frank Garcia, a point guard, was a skilled ball handler. I told the guys I wanted just Frank to handle the ball; he would be the "quarterback" of the team. As a result, we were up by two points with ten seconds left in the game. The other team called a time out. It was excruciating. There we were with only seconds remaining … and we were so close to winning. Finally, the clock started. A player from Olen, Jewel Boxstell, threw up a shot from half court, and it went in.

Luckily, the three-point play was not in effect in those days, Boxstell's shot tied the game, and we went into overtime.

After an intense battle, we won the championship by eight points.

Each year, Carbo held an annual event to raise money for agencies in the community. I would always volunteer to be a solicitor on behalf of the company, which involved asking my coworkers to donate a small portion of their earnings to various organizations such as the Red Cross, the United Way, and other non-profits. Our managers would set an annual goal, and, when that goal was met, the company would throw a party at one of the best high-class restaurants in the city. In 1975, the company exceeded their goal and threw a grand celebration dinner at John's Flaming Hearth restaurant. About seventy people attended that year, and Barney and Sig, the plant managers, sat at the head of the table.

At the beginning of the event, Barney asked everyone to stand up and give their names and where they worked. There were many buildings on the company property, and each was assigned a number, so everyone would just quickly state their name, title, and building number and then sit back down. But when it was my turn to speak, I knew I did not want to just follow the same mundane and robotic speech others had given. So I stood, and—after a long pause—introduced myself as "the black slave of the thirty-nine building."

Everyone began screaming and laughing out of control. I was only one of two people of color in the room, and while everyone knew racism was strongly prevalent within our company (and across the country), they were all shocked to hear it put so bluntly. I had been right in feeling this was the perfect time and place for humor, and was, fortunately, able to convert a rather awkward moment into one of drama, happiness, and levity. The laughter lasted for several minutes, and when the dinner was over, Sig, the plant manager, came up to me and told me to come to his office some time.

I decided to take Sig up on his offer. One day after work I went to his office. I introduced myself to his secretary and told her I was there to see Mr. Sig, who was in a meeting with his staff at the time. At the end of the meeting, his secretary brought me in.

Sig introduced me to his staff of ten men. As I walked in, he said to them quite sternly, "Men, I want you to meet the black slave of the thirty-nine building." He began laughing so hard, just the same way he had at John's Flaming Hearth. His staff was just stunned. His demeanor was straight business; he was not the kind of man who you'd think would laugh easily. Finally, when everyone saw me laughing, they laughed as well. Bob Regal, one of Sig's staff members, was on the company basketball team, and he thought it was hilarious that Sig would be so straightforward with me.

Sig thanked me for coming and later told me it had been years since he'd laughed that hard. He gave me a tour of the company and introduced me to all of the secretaries on his staff. We had a brief conversation about how the company operated and discussed some of the social issues within the company. He ended our conversation by letting me know that his door was open to me at any time or for any cause, and he remained true to his word. Sig became my friend, though I did not share our relationship with anyone.

Then, later that year, our company won the championship in basketball. Sig held a dinner for our team at John's Flaming Hearth. I gave him a championship jacket, and he was so pleased. Bob Regal said it was good timing; Sig had been going through some personal things.

Humor had once again helped me to persevere.

Make 'Em Laugh

Growing up, I discovered my own way of not running away from anything, and of perceiving and solving problems—not by confronting them so much as by diffusing them. Everyone I have ever met has had a problem or crisis that could have been solved simply by talking it through. That's why it's important to be genuine; once people know who you are, they open up to you, and it becomes easier to talk to them.

Everyone is born with gifts; they just need to know how to harness those gifts. Life is a mystery, and to navigate this mystery, both internally and externally, we must fulfill our responsibilities to ourselves and make use of the gifts we have been given.

One of my greatest gifts is humor. When I talk to people who are dealing with a problem or crisis, many times I begin with my humor. It can be a great tool if you use it in the right manner and at the right time. Humor can open doors for conversation, and getting people to talk is a key to helping them. Helping people through their issues requires patience and the ability to listen; people want to be heard. Once I have patiently listened, I use humor to make connections with people who, after a short time, begin to realize, "Hey, this guy is just like me."

I am blessed to have made people laugh so hard, they cried like babies. I have been thanked countless times by people for making them laugh when they "haven't laughed like that in a long time." It's a shame when people get so caught up with the things of the world that they don't enjoy life and laughter. When you make others feel good, you feel good also. When you lift others up, you are lifted up as well. There are always opportunities to do something good and to make things better, otherwise your world will still be stuck in crisis and full of trouble.

For example, when I worked at the South Junior High recreation center in 1975, I supervised the gym activity. One night, two white men got into an argument in front of their kids. It got to the point where it looked like there would be a physical altercation. It was my job to keep order. It could have been quite awkward, but I stepped in and said, "You know what I love about you guys? You set such a good example for your children." With that, everyone started laughing. The hard feelings disappeared, and there was a sense of community that hadn't been there before—among all of us.

⚜

My purpose in life has always been to bring happiness, joy, and peace into the lives of everyone I meet, and to make them react in unpredictable ways. I get so much joy out of making people laugh, and, after over seventy years of experience, I have become very skillful at it. I will never say or do anything disrespectful or derogatory to anyone's character, but I have found humor to be effective for diffusing tense situations, including those involving race.

Another time, years later, around 1999 or so, it was early one morning when I was walking through the mall with my brothers, Ray and Huston, and our good friend, Charles. When we finished our walk, we decided to get breakfast at a diner that was located within the mall complex. As we approached the restaurant, Ray said, "They only let three niggers in there at one time." Then he mentioned the restaurant chain had recently been sued for discrimination for not serving blacks.

When we got there, a young white lady approached to greet us. Without hesitation I asked her, "Do you serve niggers in here?" She looked shocked and confused. I don't believe she was used to a black person being so straightforward with her. She seated us and then ran into the kitchen. A few minutes later, two women from the kitchen came to our table, laughing out loud. They told us they wished more people were like us and mentioned it was the hostess's first day working there.

When I interact with strangers, I use humor as the key to unlock the door to get to the hearts of people. It doesn't always work out the way things did at the diner—people don't always laugh. But that day, I saw a key to open a door, a way to break the ice, and it worked. And even when things don't work out, I do not apologize for who I am. I use my humor with people for the edification of others, and to bring joy to peoples' lives. I know the end result will always be positive.

I also use humor with my family. I find it draws us closer together, even when I'm playing pranks. On April Fool's

Day in 1969, I pulled a joke on Dixie Lee. It was about 5:00 a.m. when I called Dixie and said our father was in Niagara Falls at Huston's house. She was so elated. As she screamed with excitement, I could barely hold my laughter. It had been years since my siblings had seen our father, and even the briefest visit with him would give them tremendous joy. After we hung up, I simply tucked myself into bed, thinking about the hilarious (some may call it cruel) practical joke I had played on my sister.

After our call, little did I know that Dixie had made calls to *all* of our sisters and brothers telling them, "Poppa is here!" Most of them got up early that morning, around 6:30 a.m., and went to Huston's house with hopes of seeing our father. They rung the door bell, waking Huston and his family, shouting, "We want to see Poppa! Sam said Poppa is here!" ... They soon realized they had been fooled, and all came to my house to get revenge. But, after all, it *was* April Fool's Day. We all had a big laugh that day and still laugh about it when the story comes up.

People are like flowers, ready to blossom and show their true beauty. All they need is love, patience, and instruction to grow. I don't use humor all the time when interacting with people, it depends on the occasion or setting. But I do believe that in life, there are always opportunities to do something good and to make things better. The world is full of trouble but you can create a world within yourself based on the way you think of yourself and others.

You are in command of that "world."

A Home of My Own

When I was just six or seven years old and growing up in Alabama, I would observe with curiosity how the lifestyles of white people and black people were so different. White people had better schools, they always seemed to drive new cars, and they owned the best and most attractive-looking homes. At such a young age, I was confused as to why my family kept moving, and why we couldn't buy a nice home just like everyone else. All I wanted was a decent place of our own.

I also noticed that white boys and girls never worked in the field or picked cotton. They went to school while many black kids worked in the fields. My mother never let us work in the fields during school, however, only when school was out, as she wanted us to get an education.

When I was fifteen years old, we were living on Mrs. Lesley Children's place near the Mayberry Gulley, where my father rented a house and farmed the land. The house was large enough for all of us (eleven people at that time), with six bedrooms—one for my parents, and five other rooms for the rest of us. My father had rented that house for over eight years by then, and I had grown accustomed to living there. But suddenly my father told us it was time to move.

That was one of many moves for my family during the next several years. Just when we'd get comfortable in a new home, we'd move again, and I was so confused as to why we were constantly moving. I didn't yet know the power of ownership, nor did I understand my parents' financial standing. Of course, my father was a sharecropper, and that required us to constantly move from farm to farm. I didn't know about economics or finance. To put it bluntly, I didn't know *anything*. So, I didn't get it; I just knew I hated it. Eventually, I came to understand that the standard of living was different for us than it was for white people—or most of them, anyway. Not all white people were rich; some white families were very poor. Finally, maybe about six months later, it clicked: my parents had not been financially able to buy a house. I made a promise to myself then that I would never rent from anybody, that I would own my home.

It was true that sharecropping was not a grand way to make a living, but I learned the importance of family; of having both parents there to raise us; of parental involvement; of a mother's love; and of a father's strength and protection—all things so many people longed for but never received. Those little things were what made our house a home. You can buy a house, but you cannot buy a home. A home is a place where there is love, trust, patience, and gentleness. I always knew I wanted each of those things—and more—for my own family.

My childhood experiences motivated me from a young age to improve my standard of living in all aspects, and as I matured, I wanted to obtain the same or even better than what I'd become used to.

At the end of 1969, Monica, Marylin, and I had to move. Sadly, the state had bought the land where we lived. The location had been so peaceful and there were no neighbors, just me, my wife, and our daughter—and Operee and her boys before they had moved to the Johnson's projects. That home was so perfect, even our driveway had a unique look, covered with brick, and there was a house next door, but no one lived there. Our small neighborhood was clean, and it was a good place to raise a family. But we had no control over the situation; we didn't own the home.

It was a Saturday morning when I received the news. I was sitting in the living room, talking with Monica, when the phone rang. It was my landlord. He called to tell me he had sold the house and property to the state. He said he was forced to sell because that area was going to be used for new development. The property was located about two miles from the American Falls, where tourists came to visit from all walks of life. The developer's plan was to build hotels, restaurants, and other businesses to accommodate the tourists.

I remember thinking to myself, *The more things change, the more things stay the same*. Life is a circle.

We had thirty days to move. I began my search by reading the newspapers, making phone calls, and driving through neighborhoods all around the city. I spent the full thirty days looking, and I could not find a place to rent. It felt inconceivable that I could soon be homeless, with nowhere to lay my head. I had a family to depend on—my sisters and brothers and my mother-in-law—but still, there was a moment in which I felt hopeless.

We were forced to put our furniture in storage and move in with my mother-in-law until we found a place to live. It was a humbling experience for me, being a man with a family and unable to provide shelter for them. My pride was shattered. I was reminded that everybody needs somebody sometimes.

Once again, it was hard to find a place to rent. Owners were mostly white and did not like to rent to black people. We stayed with my mother-in-law for about three weeks until Huston found us an apartment. The apartment was an upstairs unit with two bedrooms, a living room, kitchen, and bathroom. It was the perfect place to live *and* it was in the same neighborhood where both Huston and my mother-in-law lived.

Huston told the landlord, a white woman named Mrs. Monda, that I was a good man with a good family who needed a place to live. I went to meet her, and she rented me the apartment that same day. Although my mother-in-law and I had formed a great relationship and she had always treated me like her own son, I was thrilled to have a place for my family and myself again. And I was thankful to my brother for finding the apartment for us. I paid Mrs. Monda a month's rent in advance, and she gave me the keys the next day.

One day in 1971, after we had lived in the apartment for two years, I had just come home from work. I unlocked the door and walked upstairs to my apartment where I was met by

Mrs. Monda. She was frowning, and I knew something was wrong. She confided in me that she was behind in her taxes and could not afford to pay them. As a result, she would need to sell the house in which our apartment sat.

Then, to my surprise, Mrs. Monda asked me, "Would you like to buy this place?"

I was speechless without a single coherent thought in my mind.

Finally, I said, "Let me think about it, and I will let you know in a few days." I wasn't sure what else to say. At that time, buying a house had been the furthest thing from my mind.

And then she told me she wanted just $5,500 for the house.

All at once, it hit me. I could actually own my home. Within one day, I decided to buy the house after Raybon and Huston gave their opinions.

The next day, I went and got Raybon and Huston to look at the house and share their advice. They looked at the basement, and the first and second floors. After their inspection, they felt the house was in good condition. Both Ray and Huston owned properties, so I valued their opinions.

I bought the house that same day and—just like that—I was finally a homeowner. I was so excited to have a place I could truly call my own, and I will always be grateful to Mrs. Monda for giving me the opportunity. She lived in one of the apartments for another two years before moving out. My landlord had become my tenant, and it felt good to have that kind of control over my family's future.

It's fascinating how time brings about change. On that day in 1971, when I bought my first home, my mind cast back to Grandpa Nute. He'd endured slavery during the 1800s, a dreadful time to live as a person of color. He witnessed how families, including his own, were separated, bound with chains, and sold on market blocks. Grandpa Nute was a brave man with great courage to have survived such brutal treatment. By the time I was grown and able to afford my own home, I had begun to more deeply respect and honor my grandfather for the struggles he'd gone through. At that point, I finally understood why my father had been so affected by all the things his father had experienced.

That night, as I stood on my porch, looking at all the other homes that lined our street, it struck me that I was the *owner* of my own home. I thought to myself, *I don't have to move anymore. I can do what in the hell I want to do, because this is* my *house.* The other houses that surrounded mine were owned by white families; I was the first Black American homeowner on our street.

I remember another night that year in 1971. As I lay in my bed after a long day's work, my mind took me back to when I'd been just fourteen years old and still living in Alabama. I thought of how I'd lain in my bed all those years ago and all those states away, amazed and perplexed as I watched the fireflies flit about my room. The tiny bugs covered a large area, the lights on their tails flickering on and off in irregular but constant intervals, reminding me that there was still hope during one of the darkest periods of my young life. I can recall that mysterious sight even now. They transfixed me, gave me a vision, allowed me to hope for things I didn't have and to dream of places I'd never been.

Fourteen years later, all of my dreams had come to pass: traveling, recording music, driving a car I had bought with my own money, and coming back home to a family of my own. In a *home* of my own. I was reminded of what the King James Bible says in Hebrews 11:1: "Now faith is the substance of things hoped for, the evidence of things not seen." As a young black boy raised in the South, I had hoped to one day own a home and a car, and to raise a family of my own. More importantly, however, I'd always had *faith* those things would happen.

God answered all of my requests—and so much more. To date, I have bought three homes, two of which were built new from the ground up. I have a beautiful family and everything I could ever ask for.

It's true. Faith is the substance of things hoped for.

BACK TO THE SOUTH

In 1972, my growing family happily settled, I decided it was finally time to take that vacation to see my father. The worst of the riots in Alabama had ended, and the timing felt right. Monica had decided she didn't want to go at that time, but still, she encouraged me to go. So, instead I took Mammie Paul's son, my nephew, Willie Coleman, with me to keep me company. At fifteen, Willie was still too young to drive, but he was a great help, a joy to be around, and so excited to go with me. I gave him fifty dollars for spending money because he was not working at the time.

"Uncle Sam," he said to me, "this is going to be fun." And it was.

We planned to drive my 1967 Mustang, which was still in really good condition. I had always made sure to take care of my car by keeping up the maintenance, and I doubled checked it before we left for Alabama. We packed lightly and then hit the road around 3:00 p.m.

It was a beautiful day, the sun was shining, and it was a perfect day to travel. We were finally on our way to Alabama to see my dad.

Willie asked me, "Does Grandpa know we're coming?"

"No," I said, as a giddy smile spread across my face.

"He is going to be surprised to see us!" he said, and he grinned, his eyes sparkling the way they always do when he's happy.

When we got to Pennsylvania, we passed a section of land that was used for farming. Seeing that vast land once again took me back to my childhood, back to the fields of Alabama—my father plowing the land with his mules; my mother cooking dinner for her children; both of them working from sun up to sun down in the field, under the scorching sun. I had not forgotten the hard work and the sacrifices they had made for Willie and me to be where we were that day—speeding down the interstate in my very own Mustang. And I am still grateful today, for all the suffering they endured, because here I am, living a wonderful life because of them.

After we'd talked for hours, I looked at Willie and he was snoring. I guess my stories had rocked him to sleep and he was curled up like a baby in the passenger's seat. I drove in silence until just before the Ohio state line, when the car began to slow down. I pressed the accelerator pedal, but there was no power to increase my speed. I got off at the next exit to find a safe place to park, realizing the problem was with the engine. It was late, about 11:00 p.m. Willie was still asleep, and all the stores and shops were closed. I drove to a safe place off the side of the road, parked, locked the doors, and went to sleep.

The next morning, I woke up to a windshield covered in dew. I managed to start the engine and turned the wipers on to get a clearer view of where we were. Luckily, around 6:30 a.m., a tow truck driver saw us and asked if we needed help. I told him "yes," and explained that the car engine had stopped running due to a faulty oil pressure seal.

The man towed our car to his shop where, fortunately, he was able to replace the broken part. It took about three hours, after which I paid the mechanic $125, thanked him for his help, and we went on our way.

I drove all day and night on that second day, and we only stopped to get gas and food. As we journeyed, I had a sense of freedom, a relief of knowing that the car was in good driving condition, and it really hit me that I would see my father within in a few hours. When we entered the southern states, I warned Willie about the racism that was so prevalent in the South, and I explained to him the things we could and could not do because of the color of our skin. As I told him about how we could not drink water from the white water fountains, nor use the same bathrooms as white people, he was stunned; Willie was only fifteen years old and did not know anything about our racial history. He had been born in the North, and it was his first time in the segregated South. He had never experienced the bitterness of discrimination and was unaware of the tense race relations in that part of the country. I explained the history of African Americans in the South, and he took heed of my warnings.

We went through Ohio, Kentucky, Tennessee, and finally reached Alabama, arriving at my father's house around 11:00 a.m. on the third day. Dad was sitting on the porch, laid back in his favorite chair, with a little puppy curled up next to him. When he saw Willie and me get out of the car, he raised up and stared at us with wonder and amazement.

He was excited to see me, he was *really* excited about my car, and he was just so surprised. Dad hadn't even known

I was married, let alone that I had two daughters. We embraced each other and then went inside. Miss Polly was in the kitchen, and I hugged her as well.

He looked just as strong and healthy as before, having always taken good care of himself. The moment I saw him, I remember a small voice within my inner conscience telling me, "Take him back with you to Niagara Falls." It hadn't occurred to me previously, but in that moment, I knew it was what I had to do.

So, after we'd all talked to each other for a while, I asked Dad and Polly if they'd like to come back to Niagara Falls with us, just for a visit. I said, "Dad, all of your children are there, and they will be so glad to see you. You have grandchildren now, and great grandchildren, and it would be such a blessing for all of us to be together as a family again. What do you think?"

After a moment, he agreed, asking only for a few days to take care of business first. His response was like music to my ears, and I knew it was a prayer answered without me even having to ask the Lord. Traveling all the way to New York had been the furthest thing from Dad's mind; at seventy-four years old, the only time he'd ever left Alabama was to go to Century to see his brothers and sisters. I was really happy for him, knowing the joy he would have in seeing his growing family.

We left a few days later and were all excited about going to Niagara Falls, especially my father. It was a sixteen-hour trip from my Dad's house in Alabama to Niagara Falls, New York, and I drove the entire time, while my Dad stayed awake and talked to me. We made frequent stops; my Mustang was fun to drive, but it wasn't really designed to accommodate four people traveling up the east coast.

As I drove across the Grand Island Bridge, I was so pleased to tell my dad we were finally there. It had been such a long drive, but, oh man, we had a great time. During our long talks we really connected and fixed a lot of things, creating a newer and stronger bond that would change the whole dynamic of our family's relationship with him. And as we entered Niagara Falls, it was an extra-special moment, knowing nobody would expect to see Dad. I think it was meant to be that way.

My father had the best time of his life on that trip. He was greeted by all his sons and daughters, as well as his grandchildren and great-grandchildren, many of whom he had never seen or even heard of before. He was even able to see some friends he had grown up with as a young boy. I was so glad I had listened to that voice in my head. At the time, I'd had no idea about the impact it would have, but I was obedient. Now I believe it was God who instructed me to bring Dad up north for that once-in-a-lifetime trip.

During times like that, those special family moments, I would always think of Grandpa Nute and how he'd been taken from his family. Through the years, I've always made sure to tell his story to my children, knowing how important it is for them to understand their history. I hope they can be proud of the progress that has been made in their generation, despite the struggles our grandparents were faced with.

You must know the past to appreciate where you are today.

GIVING BACK

In 1972, I accepted a second part-time job, working for the city's recreation department. Mr. Vic Seigel was my supervisor. He knew me from my days in the Boys' Club after I had graduated from high school and before my days at Carbo. He said I could get along with anyone, which was why he hired me. I had to laugh; I am not without faults, and I profess I am no saint, but I have always tried to do unto others as they do unto me.

Mr. Seigel asked me to work at the North Junior High School, which had a program with recreational activities, like basketball and volleyball, for both youths and adults. The school was in a predominantly black neighborhood, and most households only had one parent. The program lasted from 6:00 p.m. to 10:00 p.m., with the youth period running from 6:00 p.m. to 8:00 p.m. and the adult program, from 8:00 p.m. to 10:00 p.m.

I met so many great people of all ages and ethnicities. My first night on the job, about forty boys showed up to play basketball. It was an open gym with two basketball courts, and the boys seemed like they were having fun. The next day, however, Mr. Seigel called me at home and told me some of the kids had broken into the kitchen and stolen ice-cream pops while I was on duty. I was very disappointed with myself, as I hadn't checked the doors to be sure they were locked; I'd thought it was the janitor's responsibility. I was also angry at the boys who'd broken in and made me look bad. Again, it had been my first night working there, so I didn't know any of the kids yet. To me, they were just kids playing, just young boys like I'd once been.

When I got to the gym that second evening, I opened the doors, and the boys all came inside. I immediately made them sit on the floor and told them I knew what had happened the night before. I asked them how they thought I felt, since it had been my first night working there. Then, I told them I knew exactly who'd done it. They all looked around with their eyes wide, and I just smiled on the inside. No one had told me anything, of course, but I knew it would scare them if they thought otherwise. They were all relieved when I said I was not going to turn anyone in. I then lectured them about how the white folks expected us to act out and break the rules, and how we were going to prove to them that we could conduct ourselves in a respectful manner. It felt good to share this lesson with them. All children need guidance from parents or leaders in their community, particularly children of color, who end up in juvenile detention facilities in disproportionate amounts to their white peers. Jails are not the solution, and I hoped my words could make a difference.

In the summers, when school was out, the state had a program in which college students could work and earn money during their summer vacations. That first year in my new job, I took a first-aid class along with the students in the program, as we all needed to learn how to handle emergency situations. The class was held in a large room at the recreation center. There were only two black people, myself included, in an entire group of two hundred students and teachers combined. This surprised me, given how many black college students lived in the area and needed summer jobs as well.

After the class had ended, I introduced myself to the other black man in the group. His name was Cleve Roister, and he played basketball for Niagara University. We'd later become good friends.

When I'd finished speaking with Cleve, I went to Mr. Joe's office. Mr. Joe was the manager of the recreation center. I told him I had seen only one other black person there for the summer job, but I knew many other black college students who needed jobs too. He listened to me with sincerity and thanked me for bringing the issue to his attention. He then asked me to find as many black people as I could who wanted summer jobs, and said he would hire them. I found fifteen students and, as promised, Mr. Joe gave them all jobs for the summer.

It was a great feeling to help others in need. A lot of those students hadn't known about the program, and neither had I prior to that summer. I made it my goal to ensure that every student in the area had the same opportunity to participate, regardless of class or ethnicity.

THE BLIZZARD

I've always been the person my friends and family go to when they need help. Some days it feels like my phone doesn't stop ringing with, "Sam, can you please … ?" or "Sam, I just need you to …." I'm that guy. Now, most of the time, I don't mind being that guy; I like helping others, particularly my own family. And my parents had always instructed us to help others in need. But sometimes, generosity can put you in a real mess.

In 1977, a tremendous blizzard hit Niagara Falls. It was one of the largest storms to have hit the state of New York in history. Luckily, I was off from work that week and was able to stay home. Earlier that day, the sky had been clear, and the sun had been shining. Still, the weatherman predicted that a severe thunderstorm was on the way and told everyone to be off the roads by 3:00 p.m. I took heed to the warning, and, early in that morning, went grocery shopping to buy the goods needed for my household and my mother-in-law's.

At about noon, the sky began to turn dark, and the snow began to fall hard and fast. Within minutes, you couldn't see the roads; they were covered in blankets of snow. Fortunately, my family was safe, and we were thankful to have a place to stay. By that point, all businesses were closed, and no one was permitted on the streets. So, it was quite a surprise when, at about 5:00 p.m. our phone rang. Monica answered it and told me that Aubrey Lee was stranded at the supermarket. Oh, man, I was so angry. I was especially angry at her for not calling sooner. Even still, I put on my winter coat, hat, and boots and then got in my car.

As I approached the parking lot, I saw a snowy object in the distance. I couldn't clearly tell what it was, but as I got closer, I realized it was my sister. She was completely covered from head to foot. I pulled up next to her and said, "Get in."

Aubrey Lee felt so bad, she tried to give me money, but I wouldn't accept it. After what felt like hours, we finally reached her house. The snow was still coming down, so I helped her get in safely. After getting her inside, I left to go home, and my family was so glad to see I was safe.

As soon as I had stamped the snow from my boots, I took the phone off the hook; I was not going to rescue anyone else that day.

TEACHING THE
NEXT GENERATION

As the years rolled by and we entered the 1980s, Monica; our two daughters, Marilyn and Melissa; and I continued to thrive. I was so glad to be able to give my daughters the kind of childhood I had only imagined—complete with family vacations to Washington, DC and Disney World—and it was a blessing for them to grow up around so much of their family. Our girls did very well in school, and when they entered high school, both were honor students. I was proud of them and proud of how far our family had come in just a few generations. Monica and I had always emphasized the importance of higher education, and Marilyn set a good example for her younger sister, Melissa. To this day I am still so thankful for that.

I was a member of the parents' council at their high school and attended every meeting. As a member, it was my job to support the best interests of each student and teacher by helping in any way I could. I eventually became president of the council, and my first priority was to expand our group, since there were only thirteen members. I wanted to get more parents involved. It was a hard task, but, after some time, the council grew to twenty-five members.

One day, Marilyn and Melissa came home from school and told us they had a new principal who was black. I was surprised but happy to hear it. His name was Dr. James Williams, and, to my knowledge, he was the first black male school principal in Niagara Falls, though the school taught many people of color. I went to his office to introduce myself, told him I was president of the parents' council, and explained that I had two daughters in the school. He thanked me for my involvement. Knowing Dr. Williams might face some conflict down the road, I let him know I had his back.

I later learned there were drugs in the school and grades had been going downhill, which is precisely why Dr. Williams had been hired: he was known for turning schools around. He had previously been a principal in the Buffalo, New York school system and had made great improvements with schools there. With his experience and expertise, he was able to transform Niagara Falls High School into a productive environment where students could reach their full potentials. He eliminated the school's drug epidemic, reformed its academics, and implemented a dress code. Dr. Williams created a safe environment where students could learn without distraction.

That's why I was stunned when Marilyn and Melissa came home from school one evening and told me the faculty and staff at the school were trying to get Dr. Williams fired. The teachers were even saying bad things about him to students in their classes. I knew the statements were false; it was clearly a racial issue. It appeared some of the white male teachers at the school did not want to work for a black man, so they did their best to get rid of him by making up lies about him and sharing rumors with their students. Those rumors, of course, got back to the students' parents as well.

When I got the news, I called Dr. Williams and asked, "Did you know about the rumors of you getting fired?" He said, "No." I told him to let me know if anything changed. Sure enough, a couple of days later, Dr. Williams called and said he was being terminated from his position. I told him not to worry—I would take care of it. I knew how important it was to have someone fight for you when no one else would.

I called the Niagara Ministerial Council and told them about Dr. Williams' situation, and they all agreed to help. A minister there, Reverend Raybon, set up a meeting with the superintendent Mr. Sodale, and the superintendent's deputy. I told the council we only needed three or four people to attend the meeting and deal with the matter; we didn't need a crowd. But I was overruled by another minister of the council, a weak, fearful man who would run if he saw his own shadow. This man felt that we needed a large group of ninety or more people. At this man's request, the entire ministerial council attended this meeting.

When we arrived at the board of education office downtown, refreshments had been set out for us. I was infuriated. The ministers didn't seem to realize that the refreshments and display were a tactic to try to warm us up and distract us from the task at hand. They fell for it. I, on the other hand, was not fooled. As soon as I entered the room, I shut down the talking and laughing and reminded the superintendent that we hadn't come to eat and drink. I named all of Dr. Williams' accomplishments—how he'd eliminated the school's drug problems, created a safe environment, etc.—and insisted that everyone stop undermining him. Mr.

Sodale listened as I told him flatly that everyone needed to get off Dr. Williams' back. By the end of the meeting, Mr. Sodale said he wasn't going to terminate Dr. Williams after all.

We must always stand up for what is right.

In 1987, our third daughter, Marissa was born. We hadn't planned her birth, but she was part of God's plan. Monica and I had thought we were finished with PTA meetings, track meets, tennis matches, and other responsibilities, but that all changed with the birth of our "baby" (as I've always called her) twenty years after her oldest sister was born. I like to think that parenting Marilyn and Melissa enabled me to become a better parent. And just as with Marilyn and Melissa, I found Marissa had her own personality, her own strengths and weaknesses.

Marissa was beautiful, with a strong and adventurous personality. I remember how I'd take her to a spot near the Falls to play and swing when she was two. There were always geese in the park nearby, and she loved feeding them and running after them. My baby was the blessing I needed at that stage in life; I was always on the move, so she kept me young.

CHURCH LIFE, THE
MINISTRY, AND FAITH

C hurch has always been a huge part of my life from
very early on, and it has persisted throughout my life
in many different ways. Growing up in the South,
church was especially important to my family. But our
church was more than a church—it was a meeting ground to
see friends and classmates, and a place where families from
both the surrounding towns and out in the country could
come together to worship. Ours was an all-black church, and
our congregation was all about fellowship. I still remember
everything about going to church on Sunday—the Saturday
evenings leading up to days spent in worship, getting ready
on Sunday mornings, being a part of it all, and the many
things I learned.

I can recall my church involvement as far back as the year
1948, when I was just six years old. Sunday was a sacred day,
a day of rest from the fields where farm work was done. It
was a day where food was always a big focus, and I thought
it was so much fun.

In my family, we would all get up early on Sundays and get ready for church. When I was six, we lived in a little white house my father had rented for the family, which at the time included: my mother; my father; my sisters, Aubrey Lee, Operee, Edna Jean, and Carrie May; my brothers, Eugene, AC, Raybon, and Huston; and me. With nine children in our household, some of us would take our baths on Saturday nights, and the rest of us on Sunday mornings so everyone would have time. We lived in a four-room house, with three bedrooms and a kitchen. One bedroom was for our parents, and we had separate bedrooms for the girls and us boys. In those days, our place was known as a "shotgun house," as you could open the front door and look (or shoot a gun) straight through to the back door. We took our baths in the same washing tub my mother used for washing clothes. We had no bathroom, and the washing tub was kept in the house, where we'd move it from bedroom to bedroom to take our baths.

By the time we had all finished taking our baths, breakfast would be on the table: steaming grits with butter from my father's cows, eggs, ham, homemade sausage from the smoke house, flapjacks with homemade syrup from my father's cane field, and biscuits with homemade fig and pear preserves. Then there was the coffee … its smell permeating as it sat atop the wood stove and brewed in a black, beat-up coffee pot our family had used for years. We were not allowed to drink coffee as children. It was for parents only, and my mother told us it would stunt our growth.

My mother was wise and knowledgeable about food and nutrition—and she was a remarkable cook. She always insisted we eat vegetables from her garden, particularly green foods—collard greens, turnip greens, and mustard greens—

as they were rich in enzymes and proteins. In the 1940s, those more scientific terms were unheard of, but my mother knew which food items were best for our nourishment and to help us grow up strong and in good health.

On Sundays, church was our main focus, and we would put on our best clothes. My father always dressed in a blue, double-breasted suit with pin stripes, and he'd wear a hat. My mother wore her best dress and hat. We were poor and didn't have the clothes we wanted, but used what we had. I didn't have a suit, so I wore a long-sleeved white shirt and long pants. My clothes were always neat and clean.

After getting dressed for church, all eleven of us would get in our wagon that was pulled by two of my father's mules. Riding in the wagon was not fun; it moved too slowly. My parents would always be in front on the two high, stationary seats my father had made for them. Those seats were soft and padded to make them comfortable. Then there were long benches on each side of the wagon for us children to sit on.

Our church, Mount Sinai Baptist Church, was five miles away in a little town called Gantt, which had a population of five-hundred people. Five country miles is a long distance if you consider how slowly mules walk while pulling eleven people. It seemed to take an eternity. *Click clack, click clack.* Riding alongside highway 29, cars used to zip by us so fast, the vibration shook the wagon. As a young boy, I would think about how, when I became a man, I would buy the best car made. Riding in that wagon gave me the incentive to dream.

The church was a white wooden building with a steeple on top. Inside, there was a wide, open space from the front doors to the back with pews on each side. The pulpit stood up on a platform. In the rows closest to the pulpit, the women would sit on one side and the deacons sat on the other side.

My father was a deacon at our church. That was a prestigious role in those days, and would have been comparable to something like a city council position. Dad took his role very seriously and was always so devoted to his Bible study. His bookshelf was full of Christian books, and he had a dictionary where he could look up any words he didn't understand. He also taught Sunday school and was a good teacher, always dedicated to sharing what he knew with others. My father had a way of explaining parts of the Bible in more than one way, using words that were plain and simple, so you could really get a feel for what was being said.

Sometimes my brothers, sisters and I would go to Sunday school, but more often than not, we'd play outside with our friends and socialize while our dad taught the other kids. After Sunday school, the service began and there was a devotional period. Two of the deacons would lead the congregation in hymns and then one of them would get on his knees and pray. They would pray about the pain and struggles our community experienced. The deacons prayed with such passion and sincerity that they could be heard by folks passing by the church.

After prayers, the whole congregation would sing another hymn, usually something inspirational. My mother's favorite song was, "The Lord Will Make a Way." There was no choir to sing, and there were no musical instruments—no piano, drums, or organ; people made music with their hands and feet. Still, the church members sang with an exuberance that gave anybody in attendance strong feelings of hope. I could always hear my father singing; he had such a distinct sound to his voice, high-pitched and harmonious. Many times people, often women, would become joyous and begin to shout and cheer as they felt their burdens release. There was always such a sense of victory in the sanctuary.

Reverend Chapman was our pastor. He was a great preacher who inspired us with his sermons. He was a large man, standing about six feet, two inches tall and looked to weigh about 220 pounds. The reverend never used a script when he preached; he just knew what he wanted to say, and he was powerful in his delivery. Before each sermon, Reverend Chapman would always read to us Psalms 1:1-6 from the King James Bible, "Blessed is the man that walketh not in the counsel of the ungodly, nor standeth in the way of sinners, nor sitteth in the seat of the scornful ...." He would read the full chapter, and eventually, by around age seven, I could remember the entire thing.

Psalms 1, in its entirety, is about the man who is blessed, but it wasn't until years later that I understood the third verse that said, "And he shall be like a tree planted by the rivers of water, that bringeth forth his fruit in season; his leaf also shall not wither, and whatsoever he doeth shall prosper." I took this to mean that some things are hidden from us and only revealed later, when we are mature enough to handle them. And it's true. Reading the Bible is like drinking water from the ocean: it is too large and vast to digest all at once; we must learn it sip by sip, and we will never understand it in its completeness.

My brothers and I would always sit together during service and watch the women of the congregation react to Reverend Chapman's preaching. Some would shout and wave their hands, while others wept for joy as their troubles were lifted. The men would stand and clap their hands to provide encouragement. And Reverend Chapman's sermons were so inspirational; he'd have everyone's attention.

It was years later, when rap music became popular, that I realized Reverend Chapman had actually been rapping all along. He'd put rhythm into his sermons that kept us on the edges of our seats. The whole congregation could feel it in their hearts when he shared his messages, and at the ends of his sermons, the reverend would always leave his people on high with a sense of hope to face the trials of tomorrow.

After each service was over, my parents remained in church to greet their friends. My mother would talk with other women—her friends and associates, including Mrs. Bailey and Mrs. Ware, who were good friends of hers. My sisters would go to be with Mother, hanging on her and giving her hugs, for they loved to be close to her. My father was the head deacon, and the deacons would always meet with each other at the end of service to discuss church business and community affairs.

After that all finished, it was finally time to return home, the whole service having lasted about three hours. I can remember watching people file out of the church to leave. Many would walk home, as not many people in the congregation owned cars. There were typically only two cars on the church grounds: Deacon Acey Bailey owned a Buick (he always bought Buicks), and Pastor Chapman had a Chevrolet. The rest of the families used mules and wagons for their transportation.

The mules and wagon were our only means of transportation back then, unless we rode on a mule's back. When my father had to travel a far distance, he would get a white man with a car or truck to drive him, as the mule and wagon limited the distance he could travel.

&

On the ride home from church, my mother and father would talk about the message our pastor had preached that day. And they would always remind us how proud they were to have us with them to worship together as a family. We would ride all the way back home, five miles, and I remember always thinking, *Here we go again, riding in the wagon.* I was so ashamed and embarrassed to be seen riding in that wagon. I just wanted the best things in life for me and my family.

But in 1949, that all changed. Raybon and Huston bought that 1940 Plymouth and completely transformed the dynamic of our family. They were still boys at the ages of thirteen (Huston) and fourteen years (Raybon), and were too young to have driver's licenses, but they both thought like wise old men. The boys had worked in the cotton field, saved their money, and put their earnings together. My brothers understood the importance of owning a car, and it changed our way of living in many ways. We could travel as far as we wanted, and in any weather. Raybon and Huston were two of the most remarkable young men I have ever known, and I have always been so proud to be their little brother.

Because of them, our standard of living increased to a whole new level.

&

Once per year, a revival was held at Saint Luke Methodist, a church my parents had attended when they were younger. Revivals were a large part of our church activity. Saint Luke was located in Oakey Streak on the edge of Crenshaw and Butler counties, near the city of Greenville, Alabama, and it was built by the black people of Oakey Streak in the early 1900s. Each year, we would attend the revival as a family. It became a custom for us, and it was like a family reunion, because so many of our relatives would be there: Grandpa Dunk May and Grandmom Emily Hamilton May; and my aunts, Penola Bones, Leala Florence, Berta McClain, and Ann Rose (all aunts on my mother's side). It was a great time to worship and celebrate with each other.

After the church service was over, each family brought out food. We called it "Food on the Ground." Every family had a table loaded with things like fried chicken, steak, all types of vegetables, corn, potato salad, cakes, pies, and more. There were people of all ages and of many different skin colors: black, brown, and light. All of the families would share their food with each other.

&

Years later, in 1984, I became a member of the Niagara Ministerial Council and was soon very active within the group. I served as the secretary and treasurer and was happy and willing to serve for the benefit of the council. The council was comprised of a group of about twenty pastors and ministers who would meet each Monday evening to discuss ways in which we could all foster stronger relationships between pastors and our congregations. Our hope was that this would in turn promote a better quality of life, both socially and spiritually, within our community.

During that time, there was a preacher who had moved to the city with his wife, and after being there for a few weeks, he joined one of the churches and became a member of the Niagara Ministerial Council. He was a man with a great passion for people; I think that's why we became friends. He told me about his son, who was also a minister and preached on television. His son apparently had a very large congregation.

One Sunday morning, at about 6:30, Monica and I were asleep when my phone rang. It was my new friend calling to say he was in jail and needed help. He told me he had called his pastor, but no one would help him. I told him I would be right there. I got out of bed, washed up, put on a suit and tie, and told my wife I would be back soon. When I arrived at the county jail, I greeted the lieutenant on duty, a white man who looked to be about six feet, six inches tall, and around 240 pounds. As soon as I saw him, I knew he was looking at me and thinking, *Here comes this nigger, looking for a handout. He's not going to get a damned thing from me.*

I greeted the man and said, "Good morning, sir."

Then I nodded at him, gave him my name, and told him who I was there for. He immediately replied that nothing could be done until Monday morning. So, I asked if he would please call Judge John Mariano, and he did. Judge Mariano had been a very good friend of mine for over twenty-five years. His daughter had gone to school with my girls, and he knew who I was and what I stood for in the community. When the lieutenant returned, he was much more respectful and asked me to sign the papers for my friend's release.

My friend was very glad to see me. He was sitting in the jail cell with the door open and unlocked. Apparently, he had told the lieutenant that he was claustrophobic. As I drove him home, my friend told me that had been his first time in jail. You see, his wife had falsely accused him of domestic violence. After I'd signed the papers for my friend's release from jail, the official at the desk had let me see the letter of complaint his wife had filed against him. Her words were not sensible; they were the words of a person with an unsound mind. The officer did not believe her, and neither did I. I believed my friend. My only concern at that time was for his feelings after having been locked up unjustifiably. That brief time spent in jail must have been a profound moment of suffering and torment for him.

I could see the minister wanted to talk with someone, so I took him for a long ride. He said he would never forget what I had done for him, but I had recognized this as a time when help was needed. I knew there were no perfect marriages. Even Adam and Eve had disruptions in their marriage. I wasn't there to judge, just to help.

On that particular Sunday, my ministry took place outside of church.

A New Kind of Ministry

Early on in my life, my experiences with church taught me the value of being a decent person, a person with integrity. Sure, some of this knowledge came from my father and from reading the Bible, but a good part of it was from pure life experience. I also learned how sometimes, experiences with other people show you not only what kind of person you want to be and become, but also what kind of person you do not want to emulate.

When I was a child, our preacher Reverend Chapman and one of the deacons, along with their wives, would sometimes come to our house for dinner. My mother would cook a huge meal, because she was kind, gracious, and giving. Every time, the preacher, the deacon, and their wives would eat so much food, there was almost nothing left for the rest of the family. Our family was not as wealthy as these church folks who bought new cars every couple of years, still, we found they were the types to not only eat lots of our food, but also take some home, leaving us without leftovers. Meanwhile, a few of my sisters and I didn't even have decent shoes to wear.

One time, my father, some of my siblings, and I went to Reverend Chapman's home in Troy, Alabama. Any time our family hosted a member of the church, we would cook and offer generously. But when Reverend Chapman's wife saw us kids walk through the door, she prepared just one dry, unappetizing bologna sandwich to split among the four of us. They were without shame and had no class or dignity about themselves. To me, they seemed like pigs who ate up everything without consideration for anybody else. They were only concerned for their own bellies. What a damned shame; this was not an act of Christianity. Jesus fed the people.

It was these kinds of things that made me come to realize that some of the church officials I had known since I was very young were actually not good people. I thought of how Reverend Chapman would read to us from Psalms 1:1, "Blessed is the man that walketh not in the counsel of the ungodly, nor standeth in the way of sinners, nor sitteth in the seat of the scornful ...." I have always and will always try to be a Godly man.

Not perfect, but Godly.

Even as an adult, I came to know church officials who I did not want to be associated with because I did not consider them decent people. I chose to go into the ministry despite the behavior of those types of people, people who would take advantage of others and act selfishly. I grew to have a zero tolerance policy for preachers and church officials who did not represent our faith well. Because of this, I would often bounce around to different churches with my family. I did not want any of us to be associated with corrupt and morally bankrupt people, especially church officials who we held to a high standard.

All of this nonsense could have made me question my faith, but it didn't. It only strengthened it, because it made me realize I had to take my faith seriously and continue to be a good person. More and more, I put my faith to the test, made sure to always treat people with decency, and appreciated those who also treated people the way they deserved to be treated.

Not perfectly, but in a Godly manner.

MY KIND OF MINISTRY

Finally, in 1997, I listened to the voice in my heart and began studies at the Colgate Rochester Crozer Divinity School in Rochester, New York, where I received my degree in biblical, theological, historical, and ministerial studies. The school was a theological college affiliated with the American Baptist Church, and there, one could receive the best in-depth learning imaginable.

Professor Terry Warr taught a course called Leadership Development, one that left a significant impression on me. In his class, I learned about how a solid education is key to continued learning later in life, and how strong leaders should always keep studying to stay up-to-date in their professions. Good leadership is so crucial, and I think every person in a leadership position should have to take a similiar class, particularly pastors and ministers. Ministers are people who lead their congregations in faith. They change lives. What better way to lead than through faith?

Through their admirable leadership, Professor Warr and my other wonderful teachers equipped me with a deep knowledge of the Bible, opening my eyes and spirit to things I had not fully comprehended previously. They were deep thinkers and encouraged students to dig, seek answers, and always continue their studies.

My graduation in 2001, at age fifty-eight, was so exciting for me; I had reached one of my goals—earning a college degree—by working my regular job at Carbo and attending school at the same time. School had required hard work and long hours of study, but I graduated with an A average. To me, my graduation was a testimony that if a person sets goals, focuses on what they want, and isn't distracted, they can accomplish anything.

The day I graduated from Colgate Rochester Crozer Divinity School, my family and friends were all there to celebrate with me. I felt great in the grey, Italian silk suit I had bought just for the special occasion. There were a lot of students graduating that day, and the campus wasn't big enough to accommodate everyone, so the school had to move commencement to a large church in town. There were buses lined up to transfer people to and from the graduation ceremony, and I walked to one of the bus stations on campus, where there were mostly white people sitting and waiting for a ride to the graduation site.

It was such a wonderful day, and I wanted to share my joy through humor. I walked up to the front of the group and asked the lady in charge about instructions for transportation. Of course, I already knew all the details, but I wanted to change the atmosphere to make people laugh and feel good. So, I asked her if I could ride in the front, or if I had to go to the back of the bus. Everyone was listening and watching, and I knew it. I wanted everyone's attention at that moment, because I knew they would laugh. The people around me were older, and they knew the history of the boycott in Montgomery, Alabama, when blacks had not been allowed to ride in the front of the bus, but had to ride in the back. When I asked, the lady just looked stunned and stared at me; she could not say anything. And, just as I expected, the group erupted with laughter. I felt great, knowing the atmosphere had just been lightened, and I gave them all a cheeky smile before heading to my position in line.

Minutes later, when we all boarded, people were still laughing and telling me to get to the back of the bus.

FULL CIRCLE

There was a time around 1995, during which I was still involved in the Niagara Falls Church community, when I went to see a member of our congregation, Mrs. Todd. I had gone to her home to serve her communion because she was sick and unable to attend church. When I arrived, Mr. Todd was there, and I had the pleasure of meeting him for the first time. After our introduction, he said whenever he met someone, he would "weigh" them, meaning he would judge them by their character—what they were all about and whether they were real or phony. I knew exactly what he meant. After we talked for a short period of time, I asked him how much I "weighed." Mr. Todd laughed heartily at my question. He said I was "all right," and I was pleased with his response. He was a wise man who didn't talk much, so when he did speak, his words had great substance.

Mr. Todd told me about his childhood, about being raised in the deep South, about things he had experienced as a young man, and why he had grown to never trust new people. I asked him where exactly he'd grown up, and he said Alabama. I asked him what part, and he said in the country, outside of Greenville. So, I asked him if he knew any

Carters, and he said, "Yes." Then, to my delight, he went on to name all my father's brothers and sisters. I was stunned; here was someone who had actually known Grandpa Nute! He and my dad had played together as children and grew up together. He even knew my grandmom, whom I'd never met, either. Her name was Mariah Carter. I'd never even heard her name before, because my father had never talked about her. It may have just been too painful for him to talk or even think about the inhumane and brutal treatment his parents had endured. I so wish my father could have seen Mr. Todd one more time when he visited Niagara Falls, but that was years prior, and he had passed away by the time I met Mr. Todd.

Isn't it amazing what a small world we live in? Meeting Mr. Todd was a perfect example. I went to his home to serve communion to his wife and ended up learning so much more about my grandpa's life. That day, as I sat in the Todd's living room, Grandpa Nute came alive for me in a way he never had before.

Mr. Todd told me how my grandpa would often cry at night, loudly enough for others to hear him from down the road. Apparently Grandpa Nute had gotten very sick and was all alone when he passed away. Mr. Todd remembered the subject of the sermon the preacher gave at Grandpa Nute's funeral: "Children will leave you when you get old." How unbearably sad it was to learn this. Still, I was so glad to have met Mr. Todd and to have had the conversation we did. I will always be thankful for his willingness to share with me.

Slavery still has a great impact on the lives of black people. Our forefathers suffered brutal treatment, and those scars have been passed down from generation to generation. But it is so important to remember those stories and to use them as fuel to stand up against any form of slavery that still exists. Slavery, in a way, can be found in many of our institutions—in schools, in the workplace where there are abusive and racist bosses who oppress their employees, and even in some churches.

When I read my Bible, it teaches me how to deal with all the issues I face in life, racial or otherwise. Through the Bible, I find a solution to every problem. Paul says it best in 2 Timothy 2:15: "Study to shew thyself approved unto God, a workman that needeth not to be ashamed, rightly dividing the word of truth," (King James Bible). This is right. Truth is power.

Moving Forward

I was too young as a child to understand how my grandfather's life had impacted not only my father, but also my family and me. Now I recognize the lasting effect his struggles still have and will continue to have for generations to come. Slavery is like a ripple on a pond; it spreads through generations, leaving mental and emotional scars.

It was later in my childhood, around age ten or so, that I began to notice and understand events of racism and terrorism in my community. I can still remember one moment in particular. It was 1952, when two white men drove their car up to our house in the middle of the night and began honking the horn, waking all of us up. My brother Raybon got up first and, like a brave soldier, went out and confronted them for waking us up.

It was not long before my father stepped out onto the porch, armed with his double-barreled shotgun. He shouted to Raybon, "Move back," then shot at the car, shattering the windshield. The men took off as fast as they could.

Luckily, no one was hurt or killed.

Those two men drove into a nearby town, Andalusia, and put that car on display. See, these two men owned a finance company that lent money to black people in our community and charged them with extreme interest rates. My brother Eugene had borrowed ten dollars from these men and paid them back fifteen dollars. Then he decided to borrow twenty dollars, but he had only repaid twenty dollars before he moved to Niagara Falls. Hence their arrival in front of our house.

These lenders were known for coming after people if they did not or could not pay. They showed no respect for black people and were not above raiding their homes, terrorizing families, or even committing murder. And they got away with it every time.

The next day, the sheriff came to our house and asked for Huston; they thought he was responsible for the shooting. My father, with his high level of wisdom and courage, went to the courthouse in town and told the judge the true story of what had happened, explaining that, as a man, it was his duty to protect his family. The judge agreed and told him he'd done the right thing. That finance company soon went out of business and left town to find somebody else to terrorize. After that, my father was looked at with respect by the community. He was not fearful of anyone, but respected everyone in return.

That was an inconceivable thing for a child my age to witness. Fortunately, I was blessed to have wise parents and a strong family, so this did not leave as devastating an effect on me as it could have.

For over seventy-five years now, I have witnessed the consequences of being a black man in America. From going to a segregated school in Alabama to drinking from the colored water fountain, it was all about race. Race is ever-present.

In 1968, around the time Monica and I married, I went to one of the major banks in town to ask for a loan to buy a home. This was in Niagara Falls, New York, the progressive North. I had a steady job and money in the bank, and still, they refused to give me the loan. I did not fully grasp the reason at that time. I didn't yet know that banks never lent money to blacks to buy homes. Cars, maybe. Homes, rarely.

In my life, I have been blessed to have known several people who fought back against racism, oppression, and injustice; people of all ethnicities, groups, and professions; people who made a great impact in my life and the lives of others; people with principles.

Attorney Francis Shedd was a white man who became my friend and advisor. At one point before he retired, he was the oldest attorney in the city, but he was a man with dignity and respect for all mankind. He was conscious of the fact that racism was prevalent in the city and was determined to neutralize it.

Judge John Mariano was the chief judge in Niagara Falls, who I was fortunate enough to meet through Francis Shedd. These two white men were my brothers, they treated me with great respect. Socially, I felt like we were on the same level. They became my mentors who knew and understood the social and racial issues within our city and community. Their leadership helped me to become more skillful in the high-priority situations I faced within the school system, workplace, and community. With the help of these wonderful men, I was able to get a few people who were incarcerated—like my preacher friend—released from jail on my recognizance. Judge Mariano was abundantly aware of and understood how our country's racial justice system was not fair to people of color. So, he was supportive of my efforts to ensure that those without voices received justice amidst their crises.

Dr. C.C. Booth was a black man who was my physician, my friend, and my mentor. He was more than a medical provider; he was a humanitarian who was concerned about the lives and the welfare of people. Dr. Booth once told me how, early in his medical career, when he had first started his practice in Niagara Falls, a senior doctor had not received him well and was very open about his dislike for him. This gentleman made every effort to prevent Dr. Booth from becoming successful ... all because he was a black man.

Dr. Booth became one of the leading doctors within our city.

Years later, when that doctor who had done Dr. Booth so bad got sick, his family put him in a nursing home. That doctor's son asked Dr. Booth to take care of him. Being the great man that Dr. Booth was, he cared for that man until the day the old man passed away.

❧

I am inclined to believe that there will always be racism and injustice in America. There are some people who are simply incapable of doing what is just. Racism is a disease that has no cure. It is a behavior that divides and alienates people, driving us away from each other and keeping us from being effective or living meaningful lives. Like a cancer, it destroys people—and it needs to be treated.

My parents taught me good principles to live by. First, they taught me to have respect for myself and for others, and to never be afraid to speak out about things that were unjust. Second, they told me to always approach situations in an appropriate way, and to always show concern for other people and their struggles. And third, they explained to me the importance of good character, how my character would follow me through my entire life, and how I was in control of and responsible for my own destiny. It was precisely because of their lessons and the history of our ancestors that, as a young boy, I began to dream. I dreamt about the life I wanted—a life of respect and compassion for myself and for others.

Everything I wanted in life, I've achieved.

Life is a gift from God. No person or institution has the right to control or dictate the course of one's life. Every person on this earth has the right to choose their own destiny, but we must have the will and the determination to fight for what is ours. And we must fight for those who are unable to fight for themselves, as well. Life is a bit like being a butterfly; your experiences create a cocoon around you, but your personal growth helps you to release yourself from that cocoon so you can spread your wings and fly. It is only through that release that you discover your real self.

So, if you want to know who *I* really am: I am someone who is authentic and simple. I am someone who loves

God and my brothers and sisters of *all* races—black, white, Hispanic, Asian, and others. I do not put myself above or below anybody else, because we are all created of the same dust. I am someone who treats everyone the way I want to be treated. And because of those who came before me, I am my own someone.

This is who I am and who I will always be.

Samuel Carter, Grandson of a Slave

Samuel Carter, age twenty, 1963

◁ *Dad, sitting on his porch in Alabama before Willie and I took him to Niagra Falls*

My father, Aubrey Carter, ▷ age seventy five, during his visit to Niagra Falls in 1972

Dad wears a new suit gifted ➤
to him by the Carter sons

My parents' family church in ⌄
Pigeon Creek, Alabama

My mother, Essie Arnel May Carter, in 1952

My maternal grandparents, Dunk May (left) and Emily Hamilton May